A Time to Teach,
A Time to Dance

A Creative Approach To Teaching Dance

Margaret De Haan Freed

J P

JALMAR PRESS, INC.

Library of Congress catalog card number: 76-19647
ISBN: 0-915190-04-4
Printed in the United States of America

Edited by Helen M. Friend
Designed by John T. Bookout
Photos, unless otherwise credited, by Alex Ortiz

Cover photo by Alex Ortiz
Cover design by John T. Bookout

TABLE OF CONTENTS

ILLUSTRATIONS

Acknowledgements

My thanks are extended to several generations of dance students who have experienced and experimented with the ideas described in *A Time to Teach, A Time to Dance.* Among my most recent and most outstanding students, deserving special mention and appreciation are Debra Ayres, Alice Fong, Carleen Gamick, Pamela Johnson, Julie Nemes, and Leslie Oakham, who posed for the photographs in the book.

To the many, many dance teachers under whom and with whom I have worked, especially the late Ruth Whitney Jones, to whom this book is dedicated.

To my husband, Alvyn M. Freed, without whose encouragement, support, insistence, assistance, criticism and love, this book would never have seen the light of day.

To my son, Jesse Mark Freed, who suggested the title of the book and supported my efforts with his interest

To Alex Ortiz for his photography and his ability to catch the spirit of dance on paper.

To Mrs. Sandi Willard for her patience in preparing the manuscript—over and over again.

To Mrs. Edythe Rogers for her review of the original concepts for the book and her helpful suggestions.

To Mr. John Adams, Editor of Jalmar Press, Inc., for his invaluable assistance and general competence.

To Ms. Helen Friend, a friend indeed, for her outstanding work in editing the book and in helping to clarify my ideas.

To Mr. John Bookout who put it all together, as the imaginative designer.

My indebtedness to all these people is clear, and I acknowledge their indispensable contributions with a heartfelt thank you.

Introduction

Of the many fine books on modern dance, few are concerned primarily with students and teachers in high school. *A Time to Teach, A Time to Dance* is intended to fill this need; it is written for secondary school dance specialists and physical educators who teach dance.

There are also a number of excellent books on the history of dance which provide the high school dance teacher with information and background in the cognitive (knowledge) domain. A number of other books list and describe a variety of techniques, emphasizing the psychomotor (physical) development. No attempt is made in the present text to duplicate such books by reviewing dance history or by including an exhaustive (and exhausting) collection of techniques.

However, dance, as a creative art experience, goes beyond technical proficiency; the emphasis in this text is placed on the creative use of movement rather than on dance history or dance technique.

In the creative area of dance, there are few practical texts for teachers. As a result this aspect of dance is too often minimized. The present text attempts to develop and encourage more creativity in teaching modern dance. The emphasis is on helping teachers to motivate students towards creativity in their classes, a little at a time.

The affective domain (the area of feelings, attitudes and creativity) is assuming ever-increasing importance while most teachers feel least able to contend with it, in specific terms. Perhaps more than any other activity in the physical education curriculum, modern dance is suited to dealing directly with the affective domain. A creative activity for groups, as well as for individuals, will produce, naturally, innumerable occasions for dealing with feelings and attitudes.

A Time to Teach, A Time to Dance supports the concept that creativity is possible for all students: that all students can learn to use movement in a creative manner through experience. To draw an analogy: a large majority of all high school graduates can write an intelligible paragraph or composition. They all start by learning letters, combining letters into words, words into sentences, sentences into paragraphs, and so on, until one of them, perhaps, writes the great American novel.

Creativity in dance also follows a regular sequence. Learning movements (letters), putting them together in sequence (words), adding variations (adjectives and adverbs), expressing meanings (ideas) is similar to writing a composition or paragraph. Dance has an advantage over other creative activities in that it presents few limitations in terms of expense or equipment: everyone has the instrument (the human body) and is familiar with the medium (movement). Many teachers claim that if a student can walk, she can dance. Some will be better dancers in terms of technique or in terms of creativity, but all can profit from the considerable benefits of the dance experience.

The vocabulary of dance is movement, and movement is affected by the time and space in which it exists. In order to use movement creatively—that is, to compose and choreograph even the shortest dance studies—it is necessary to understand this vocabulary. Part One will define and explain movement, space, and time terms. The rest of the book expands on the use of this vocabulary for creative work.

The range in availability and breadth of dance offerings in high schools will vary tremendously from large cities to rural communities. In a city school, two or more specialists in dance may offer ten dance classes throughout the year. In a small high school where there is only one physical education teacher, the total offering in dance may consist of a single unit during the year. The value of this book will be determined largely by the experience or lack of experience of the dance teacher, regardless of the amount of time the students are able to devote to the classes. It is hoped that all teachers will find some valuable material to supplement their previous experience and background.

The instructor of a semester- or year-long course will find in the text an ample number of different creative approaches from which to select her material. For a four- to eight-week unit in modern dance, the teacher will be able to use only a few of the approaches to creative work suggested, selecting the ones that seem most appropriate for *her* students, *her* school, and the time of year.

Although most high school dance teachers and students are female, more men are becoming interested in teaching dance and more male students are enrolling in co-ed classes. However, contrary to literary tradition, female pronouns will be used throughout the text to include both sexes.

A Time to Teach, A Time to Dance is a beginning, a springboard from which teachers and students can project themselves into the unknown realm of creative movement. Words are not adequate. The thrill of creating and the joy of dancing can only be experienced.

PART ONE

The Vocabulary of Dance

Chapter One
Movement Classification

All human movement may be classified as locomotor, axial, or a combination of the two. This classification covers not only dance movement but all the natural or learned activities which people perform.

LOCOMOTOR MOVEMENT

Locomotor movement moves through space, over a moving base. It means going somewhere, from one place to another. The usual base is the feet but it need not be: locomotion is also possible while the weight rests on the hands, the knees, all fours, hips, back, or stomach. For the purpose of dance, we usually consider eight fundamental or basic locomotor movements:

1. *Walk*—transfer weight from one foot to the other, with at least one foot always in contact with the floor.
2. *Run*—transfer weight from one foot to the other, with a moment when both feet are off the floor simultaneously.
3. *Leap*—transfer weight from one foot to the other, the transfer of weight occurring in the air; the moment in which both feet are off the floor is prolonged.
4. *Hop*—take off from one foot and land on same foot.
5. *Jump*—take off from both feet and land on both feet.

These five basic locomotor movements are executed in an even rhythm: only a single beat is required for each one.
The following three basic movements are performed in an uneven rhythm—a long and a short (♩ ♪) beat are needed to complete a single movement.

6. *Skip*—step and hop in an uneven rhythm, changing feet on each step.
7. *Slide*—step and close sidewards in an uneven rhythm, the transfer of weight taking place in the air.

Fig. 1.   A leap is an exuberant movement.

8. *Gallop*—step and close forward or backward, in an uneven rhythm, the transfer of weight taking place in the air. Same foot continues to lead.

Locomotor movements may be combined into patterns for variety and interest. All students seem to enjoy the fast, vigorous activity of these movements (watch the eyes light up and the smiles break out). Practice in locomotion provides excellent contrast to more "serious" or strenuous techniques.

The fundamental locomotor movements may provide a starting point for creative work in dance. Steps from folk dance (such as schottische, polka, mazurka) or steps from past or present social dances (such as waltz, tango, or rock) also may be the starting point for a dance or suite of dances, Saturday Night Hoe-Down or South American Suite, to suggest two.

(See Part Two of this book for more detailed suggestions for the use of loco-motor movements as a stimulus of dance composition.)

Fig. 2. A skip may involve either elevation or distance.

AXIAL MOVEMENT

Axial movement may be defined as movement *in* space over a fixed base. In simple terms, axial movement is performed in place, using the torso rather than arms or legs. It is in this area of movement that modern dance departs most drastically from ballet. Movement is centered in the torso and follows through into the extremities. The range of body movement possible is limitless and provides opportunities for extensive experimentation in which the students determine their own capabilities.

Axial movement can be classified in many ways: stretching and bouncing, pushing and pulling, rising and falling, lifting and dropping, contracting and expanding. Each teacher may wish to determine her own classification or terminology but the following classification is a convenient, clear, and precise one, based on the way force or energy is directed and controlled in the body movement.

1. *Sustained*—a long, continuous application of the same degree of force with no differentiation between impetus and follow-through. (Example: push, pull, reach, stretch.)

2. *Swinging*—impetus is a tipping off balance (a pulse) and the follow-through is a long arc or curve, following the pull of gravity. Swings may be pendular, circular, figure 8, or combination. (Example: swaying, arm swing, leg swing, body swings.)

3. *Percussive*—explosive impetus, little or no follow-through. (Example: striking, beating, bouncing, falling.)

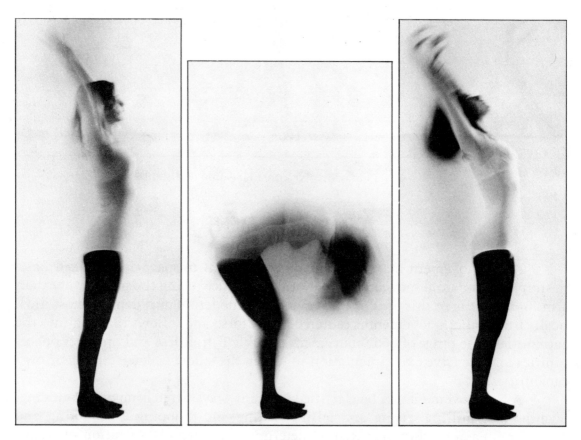

Fig. 3-5.   A down and up two-beat swing shown in three stages of movement.

Many movement sequences and techniques combine two or more of these forms of axial movement. A percussive fall may be preceded by a swinging preparation and followed by a sustained recovery.

A bounce-and-stretch series will combine percussive body bounces with sustained body stretches.

Some dancers consider the following as separate types of movement, but in this book they will be treated as variations of the three basic axial categories: vibratory, suspended, contraction and release, to name a few. These are special kinds of application of force, special techniques to learn and practice but each is a part of one of the larger categories of axial movement.

Vibratory movement is a series of short, quick, percussive movements, performed in rapid succession. Suspended movement incorporates a feeling of "breath" or "lift" to hold the body in the air. There may be a percussive impetus followed by a sustained follow-through or a sustained impetus followed by a percussive collapse as the "breath" is expelled. The feeling of "breath" may be achieved by practicing inhalation and exhalation: inhale quickly and exhale slowly or inhale slowly and exhale quickly, letting the body lift with the inhaled breath and collapse on the exhaled breath.

Fig. 6.   Contraction and release.

Contraction and release are terms which Martha Graham, America's premiere dancer, has made popular. Contraction involves a pulling together of the ribcage and pelvic girdle; the release is stretching them apart again. Graham uses these two movements as the basis of her dance. However, contraction and release may be performed either with percussive or sustained energy flow.

Chapter Two
Space Factors

Movement exists in both time and space. The body, whether in motion or in repose, has volume and fills space in three dimensions. A piece of sculpture or a painting also exists in space; music exists in time. Movement cannot exist without both elements. This being true, the way in which the many possible variations of time and space are organized becomes central to a creative use of movement to develop dances.

A simple exposition of space elements follows, while suggestions for their use as basic choreographic stimuli are included in Part Two.

DIRECTION

In performance, direction has two aspects in regard to *locomotor movement:* the direction the body is moving and the direction the body is facing in relation to the stage or to the audience.

1. *The body can move* forward (front of body leading), backward (back of body leading), or sideward (right or left side of body leading). Diagonal movement combines forward and sideward or backward and sideward directions and involves a twist of either the upper or lower trunk to produce a true diagonal focus of the body. Turning movement combines the various leading surfaces of the body.

2. *Direction in reference to the stage* or audience is based on the traditional stage description:

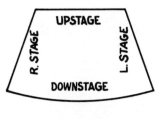

AUDIENCE

When a dancer moves downstage she moves toward the audience. A dancer may move forward downstage (front of body to audience), backward downstage (back to audience), or sideward downstage (left or right side to audience). Forward, backward, sideward, or diagonal movement may also be performed toward all of the other stage areas.

3. *Combining body and stage direction.* A moment's thought will reveal how many different patterns of walks, for example, could result from the assignment "Walk a square on the floor." The floor pattern would be the same for all, let us say

(1) 4 walk steps downstage

(2) 4 to R stage

(3) 4 upstage

(4) 4 to L stage

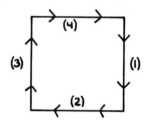

One pattern might be all forward walks, including 4 quarter turns at the corners;
One pattern might be with the body facing downstage throughout: 4 forward, 4 sideward R, 4 backward, 4 sideward L;
One pattern might be all backward walks, including 4 quarter turns.

You can see that the combinations of body direction plus stage direction possible in even such a limited problem become quite extensive. When variations in floor pattern are added (that is, where the dancers go on the floor), it becomes even more apparent how one simple space factor (direction in locomotion) can add interest and variety to the simplest movement.

Direction in axial movement takes in more three-dimensional considerations than does direction in relation to locomotion. In this case, movement may be vertical, horizontal, diagonal, curving, or spiral. The direction of axial movement refers to the *shape* or contour of the body in space. A single body may have a low or high contour, a contracted or extended shape, a twisted or curved shape. When you combine the shapes of several single bodies together to create the contour of a group of bodies, you open the door to an infinite variety of expressiveness.

LEVEL

As the word itself suggests, contour is partly a matter of the use of *level*, but since changes of level also occur in locomotion, level can be considered as a distinct and separate element of space. The body can move from the lowest possible level (lying on the floor) to highest (elevation from the floor) including use of stage properties or sets to increase height above floor. The lift of one dancer by another (as in ballet "pas de deux" or in gymnastic pyramid building) represents one type of extreme level changes.

1. *In locomotor movement,* flexed knees, rounded body, and flexed hips provide a low level. Jumps or leaps, moving on tip-toe with extended body and arms overhead represent the highest levels. A contrast between high and low levels of movement can add interest to the simplest of locomotor patterns.

2. *In axial movement,* change of level can be achieved in each of the different starting positions: lying, sitting, kneeling, and standing. Infinite variations on each of these positions are possible.

Fig. 7.   Several lying positions showing variations in use of body, arms, legs, and tension.

a. In lying, one is either on the front, back, right side, or left side— but the positions of arms, legs, and head can be changed in relation to the torso. The degree of tension or relaxation in the body or any part of the body can vary even a fundamental lying position.

b. Sitting positions are those in which one or both hips are supporting the body's weight. From practicing techniques, the student will have learned these basic sitting positions:

(1) Frog sit: soles of feet together.
(2) Long sit: both legs extended forward.
(3) Stride sit: both legs extended diagonally forward.
(4) Hurdle sit: both legs flexed at knees, one leg in front of body, other leg toward back.
(5) Half-hurdle sit: one leg flexed, one leg straight.
(6) Hook sit: knees flexed, feet on floor.
(7) Half-hook sit: one leg flexed with foot on floor, other leg extended as in long sit.
(8) Tailor sit: legs crossed.

Fig. 8. From left to right, half-hurdle sit, long-sit, stride sit, and frog sit.

Each of these basic sitting positions can be used as a starting position for axial movement and each can be varied by changing the position and relationship of body, head, and arms to the sitting base.

c. Kneeling positions give the dancer more freedom of movement than do lying or sitting positions, because the base is smaller (one or both knees), allowing for more flexibility in the relationship of torso and arms to the base.

Once again, the techniques practiced for body control and movement exploration will have familiarized students with the fundamental kneeling positions. These include:

(1) Kneel stand: body upright over knees.
(2) Kneel sit: body sitting on heels.
(3) One leg kneel stand or sit: second leg extended sideward, forward or backward.

At the kneeling levels, the torso may be upright, rounded forward, twisted to either side, leaning backward or sideward, while the arms may be used to accentuate or contrast with the body position.

Fig. 9. From left to right, two kneel stands, a one-leg kneel stand, and kneel sit.

d. The highest natural stationary level is, of course, the standing position. This also allows for infinite variations in position of legs, torso, and arms. The weight may be centered over both legs or over one. The knees may be flexed or extended; the torso may be upright, rounded forward, tilted, or twisted sideward. The arms may be at the dancer's sides, lifted forward, sideward, or overhead at various levels. Both arms may be in the same position or assume different positions.

Fig. 10. Several standing positions showing variations in use
of parts of the body, focus, and tension.

It may seem strange that the discussion of level in axial movement is so
much more extensive than in locomotor movement, but a moment's thought
should make the reason obvious—changes of level are much more common in
axial movement than they are in locomotor. They are more extreme. You don't
do too many locomotor movements lying on the floor. You do some—you crawl
around—but even that's basically axial movement. Most locomotor movement is
done from a standing position and the variations occur in body direction. Level
and axial movement are more closely related in natural human movement as well
as dance. But whether it is axial or locomotor movement, level is a vital aspect
of space to consider in relation to movement variations.

FOCUS

Focus is another element of space which can be used to vary the meaning and impact of movement. Focus is the central point of attention and generally means the direction of the gaze. Perhaps more importantly in dance, it may also refer to the directing of a body or a group in a specific direction or toward a specific location. You can think of focus as an imaginary magnetic pole which governs the attention and action—attracting or repelling, but always a very real felt force. Focus may be in the same, opposite, or contrasting direction in relation to movement.

A few examples will suffice to show how focus can add an extra element of meaning to movement. A shifting focus may indicate indecision, or uncertainty. A downward focus may indicate sorrow; a backward focus may indicate fear. The instructor should emphasize that the whole head or body should indicate the desired focus, not just the eyes, since an audience cannot always see the eye position clearly enough to understand the intended meaning.

RANGE (AMPLITUDE)

One other space factor should be mentioned at this time, with further suggestions on creative use included in Part Two. Amplitude (or range) of movement means the size of the movement, from small to large. A single movement, either locomotor or axial, can encompass a tremendous range and in so doing communicate a variety of meanings. Movement can build from small to large for a climactic effect; large movement by a group can contrast with a solo figure for an entirely different meaning.

It may take some experimenting on their own for students to learn the effects of manipulating this element. To begin with they won't think of changing the size of a movement. If they're going to do a movement four times, they'll do the movement the same way four times and move on to something else. Taking a single simple movement such as a circle with the hand and making a small, medium, large, and very large circle will increase the interest of repetition— an added value is getting the students to realize they can double the amount of material they have through *development* of ideas instead of just stringing embryonic notions together.

Chapter Three
Time Factors

Dance exists in time as it does in space—the passage of time from the beginning to the end of a movement, a technique, a pattern, or dance is inevitable. The organization or structure of time in dance, or in music, is called rhythm (and if ever a word is commonly mis-spelled or misunderstood by students, it is this one! RHYTHM!)

Our lives are built on natural rhythms: the beat of the heart, the regular inhalation and exhalation of breathing, the cycle of sleeping and waking, the act of walking. Therefore, rhythm is not foreign to our bodies. An increased awareness and understanding of the various elements of rhythm, as used in music and dance, will enable the student to work more effectively in creating dances, with or without musical accompaniment. This section will briefly explain basic rhythms and rhythmic devices with a further exploration of their use as creative springboards in Part Two.

METER

Meter refers to the underlying beat of music or dance, the organization of accented and unaccented beats into repetitive series, called measures. The most common meter is ¼, 4 beats to a measure, with a quarter note receiving one beat and the accent normally falling on beat 1: ♩ ♩ ♩ ♩ |

Other common meters are ¾ ♩ ♩ ♩ |

²⁄₄ ♩ ♩ |

⁶⁄₈ ♪ ♪ ♪ ♪ ♪ ♪ | ♪♪♪ ♪♪♪

Contemporary composers (of both music and dance) may use less common meters for interest and variety.

⁵⁄₄ ♩ ♩ ♩ ♩ ♩ |

⁷⁄₈ ♪♪♪ ♪♪ ♪♪♪ or ♪♪♪ ♪♪♪ ♪♪

Students should be able to recognize the common meters after a little practice in listening to music or to drumbeats. One method of learning is to *clap* the accented beats, then to divide the time between the accents into even beats and then to clap both the accented and unaccented beats.

Meter is sometimes called a primary rhythm and note pattern is then known as secondary rhythm. Meter (or primary rhythm) refers to the number of beats to a measure; note pattern (or secondary rhythm) refers to the way in which the basic beats are divided or arranged.

The amount of time the basic beat is given is arbitrary—you can't tell by listening whether something is $\frac{4}{4}$ or $\frac{4}{8}$.

RHYTHMIC PATTERNS

Within each measure of any meter, various rhythmic patterns may be used, meaning the way the beats are divided or combined. Rhythmic variations are essential in movement as in music; to achieve a basic understanding of note value and rhythmic patterns is a most useful tool.

1. *Note Values.* 1 measure or 4 beats of $\frac{4}{4}$ meter may be:

> 1 whole note 𝅝
> 2 half notes ♩ ♩
> 4 quarter notes ♩ ♩ ♩ ♩
> 8 eighth notes ♫ ♫ ♫ ♫
> or any combination of these which add up to 4 beats.
> Here are a few examples:

$$\frac{4}{4}\ \, ♩\, ♫\, ♩\, ♩\, |\, ♫\, ♩\, ♩\, |\, ♩\, ♩\, ♫\, ♩\, |\, 𝅝\, |$$

In musical notation, if a dot (.) follows a note, half of its value is added to that note: ♩. is one and a half beats instead of 1 beat, 𝅗𝅥. is 3 beats instead of 2 beats. Many students have already learned these basic values and need only to review and apply them to movement.

2. *Counting.* Frequently it is necessary for teachers and students to "count out" measures, rhythmic patterns, or phrases of movement or accompaniment in order to achieve accuracy of rhythmic structure. Accuracy is the key word here: musicians have been known to go into shock at what they call "dancer's counting." For example: the measure $\frac{3}{4}$ ♩ ♫ ♩ might be counted (incorrectly) by a dancer as 1 2 3 4 when there are really only 3 beats in a measure. A divided quarter (♩) note or (or two ♪ notes) should be counted as 1 &, 2 &, 3 &. The above measure would be properly counted as

♩	♫	♩
1 (&)	2 (&)	3 (&)

with the beat (1) and the (&) each receiving half the value of an ordinary quarter note.

In counting measures (to determine how long a phrase or composition is, for example) another simple device is helpful. Instead of saying "one" on the first beat of each measure, substitute the number of the measure: i.e.: <u>1</u> 2 3; <u>2</u> 2 3; <u>3</u> 2 3; <u>4</u> 2 3; etc.
3. *Phrases.* Musically and in movement, measures are usually organized into phrases, as words are organized into sentences. A musical phrase is a relatively complete musical thought; the punctuation, to refer back to our literary allusion, may be a comma, semi-colon, colon, or period. Phrases within a composition are usually equal in length: a 4 or 8 measure being the most common. The example of a rhythmic pattern on p. 18 is a 4 measure phrase. The line of a phrase may be drawn as

and may be thought to follow the line of a breath. The end of a phrase in movement may be thought of as a breath point in a dance.

To refer back to our counting dancers, students should be encouraged to count measures in terms of phrases:
Example: <u>1</u> 2 3 4, <u>2</u> 2 3 4, <u>3</u> 2 3 4, <u>4</u> 2 3 4
<u>5</u> 2 3 4, <u>6</u> 2 3 4, <u>7</u> 2 3 4, <u>8</u> 2 3 4
then to start over again with measure *one.* The number of phrases in movement or music can be tallied on a chalkboard, a piece of paper, or the always-reliable fingers of the hand.

TEMPO

Ask almost any non-musician for a definition of "tempo" and the first answer will usually be "time," probably from some memory of the word in Latin or Spanish (remember: "tempus fugit"—time flies?). Musically, tempo means *rate of speed.* The tempo used will help to determine the effect of the music or movement: in a walk, for example, a slow tempo may produce a funeral procession or a stately court dance while a brisk tempo may result in a hurrying crowd or a frantic search. Experience in moving to different tempos or to changing tempos will help students to listen and to respond to what they hear.

RHYTHMIC DEVICES

Both music and dance employ rhythm in many ways far beyond the basic rhythmic structures already mentioned. There are a few rhythmic devices used mainly by dancers in addition to more familiar musical devices, such as counterpoint, syncopation, and changing meters.

Counterpoint means the use of two or more contrasting "voices" used simultaneously. It has been used for centuries by classical composers. Students who need a more concrete explanation at this point should be directed in a four-part round like "Row, row, row your boat." In improvisational dance, counterpoint offers an interesting background for different but related movements. This will be discussed more on **p. 61.**

Syncopation refers to displaced accents, or accents occurring on normally unaccented beats or parts of beats. It is the basis of jazz music and jazz dance and will be discussed in the chapter on Jazz as a creative problem.

The two devices based on metrical changes which seem to be peculiar to dance are *accumulative meter* and *resultant meter.* Both are interesting for rhythmic variety and for their use in creative work.

An accumulative meter means the regular increase of beats per measure. Example:

♩ | ♩♩ | ♩♩♩ | ♩♩♩♩ | ♩♩♩♩♩ |

Each measure is written in a different meter: a $\frac{1}{4}$, $\frac{2}{4}$, $\frac{3}{4}$, $\frac{4}{4}$, $\frac{5}{4}$. Each measure could be repeated more than once and the meters could be increased as far as desirable. The reverse of an accumulative meter may be called a diminishing or decumulative meter and may be used separately or with the accumulative.

♩♩♩♩♩ | ♩♩♩♩ | ♩♩♩ | ♩♩ | ♩ |

One enjoyable combination is as follows:

♩ | ♩♩ | ♩♩♩ | ♩♩♩♩ | ♩♩♩ | ♩♩ | ♩ |

The pattern, performed once, totals 16 beats, or 4 measures of $\frac{4}{4}$ meter. Used with a strongly rhythmic $\frac{4}{4}$ accompaniment, the accumulative and diminishing meters provide excitement and surprise.

The *resultant rhythm,* or more accurately the *resultant meter,* is produced by the simultaneous use of two different meters, taking the accents from both. For example: Combining $\frac{2}{4}$ and $\frac{3}{4}$ meters

$\frac{2}{4}$ ♩♩ | ♩ ♩ | ♩♩

$\frac{3}{4}$ ♩♩ ♩ | ♩ | ♩♩

The resultant would be a $\frac{6}{4}$ (the number of beats required before a repetition would occur) with a strong accent on 1 and lighter accents on beats 3, 4 and 5.

$\frac{2}{4}$ ♩♩ | ♩♩ | ♩♩

$\frac{3}{4}$ ♩♩♩ | ♩♩♩

$\frac{6}{4}$ ♩♩♩ ♩♩♩

A $\frac{3}{4}$ and $\frac{4}{4}$ combined would produce a $\frac{12}{4}$ measure with accents on beats 1, 4, 5, 7, 9 and 10.

The resultant makes a neat rhythmic pattern, one which would be useful with the counterpoint previously mentioned. Working with such unusual devices provides excellent rhythmic training—important to all dancers—as well as additional means of improving choreography.

RHYTHMIC FORMS

Form provides the skeleton or structure on which compositions are built. Frequently forms used for musical compositions can be used for dance composition. Phrases are the basis for these structures. Since the phrases may be short or long, the resulting compositions will vary in length from the shortest elementary patterns to extended advanced composition.

The simplest form is the single phrase (A)—a single statement of movement. The two-part song form (A-B) is the familiar verse and chorus, two phrases. A three-phrase form could be described as A-B-C, with each phrase a different statement of movement or idea. A more common three-phrase form is A-B-A, in which the repetition of the first phrase may be the same as the first A or varied slightly. Practice in these simple forms—as in locomotor patterns or a technique series— will help the students become accustomed to working in *form* for composition. (The opposite of a composition with form is the kind of "recipe" dance students are all too likely to produce: take 2 of these and 4 of these and 2 of those and 8 of the other and just continue adding movements without any structure.)

Longer musical forms appropriate to longer dance compositions include canon, rondo, and theme and variations. These forms can be used as abstract problems in form or as the vehicle for expressing ideas or emotions with the form as a secondary consideration.

Canon—is the familiar round form, with several voices repeating the same phrases, starting at different times. Care should be taken that the succeeding phrases of the composition blend as well as contrast when they occur simultaneously.

Rondo form—is based on a repetition of the first phrase after each succeeding phrase as:
A-B-A-C-A-D-A-E- and so on.
This is a useful device for an extended composition and for manipulating material to the greatest extent.

Theme and variations—has been used for centuries by musical composers; many fine examples are available in both classical and contemporary music. A single theme is stated (in music or movement) and the subsequent sections are variations of the original theme. The variations may be in terms of tempo, rhythm, style, level, or emotional color, to name a few.

Chapter Four
Dynamics

Variety is one of the essential elements of all aspects of life. Imagine a room in which walls, carpets, drapes, furniture, and accessories were all the same color. A designer or competent homemaker would immediately demand accents of contrasting color or texture to break the monotony and add variety. Imagine a meal composed of cream soup, mashed potatoes, and vanilla pudding. Aside from the poor nutritional aspects, it would be sickening because of the lack of contrast in texture and color. Variety is not only the spice of life: it is a necessary factor for a well-balanced and interesting dance.

Fig. 11.   Dynamics determines whether movement is smooth or sharp.

In dance, dynamics refers to the flow of energy or the force expended in movement and to the way in which the force is applied. In music, the term refers to the intensity or volume of tones: intensity is indeed an aspect of energy in movement also.

The range of possible movement dynamics is tremendous: from smooth and flowing to sharp and percussive, from strong to weak, from hard and loud to soft and gentle. Accented and unaccented beats in music and in dance are differentiated by the way in which energy is directed. Movement with a pulse or impetus is characterized by an initial flow of energy with a follow-through which dissipates the energy. Another impetus or pulse is needed for the movement to continue.

The use of varied dynamics can help the dancer avoid monotony; it also provides one of the most expressive elements of dance. A pattern of slow sustained movement needs the contrast of quick, sharp accents, perhaps a sudden change of direction, or a percussive thrust of an arm or leg, or a sharp fall. A pattern of percussive beats would soon become monotonous without contrasting dynamics: a suspension turn or a long sustained pull or lift or drop.

In movement, the *amount* of energy expended determines whether a movement is strong or weak. The *way* the energy is applied to the movement determines if it is smooth or sharp. A general misconception is that movement must be soft and smooth in order to be graceful. A better definition of graceful movement is efficiency: achieving the greatest result with the least effort.

Although tempo (rate of speed) is an element of time, tempo and dynamics are closely related. Tempo ranges from slow (lentamente) to fast (presto). The combinations of energy flow and tempo provide many variations in quality and emotional content.

Movement may be slow, smooth, and strong (high tension) or slow, smooth, and weak (low tension). Fast movement may be smooth and strong or sharp and strong. Dynamics range from smooth to sharp, from strong to weak; in musical terms from legato to staccato and from fortissimo to pianissimo. The symbols

diminuendo   crescendo

indicate a gradual decrease or increase in volume, loud to soft and soft to loud.

Individuals all have their own natural energy flow; watch a stream of pedestrians for a while and you cannot avoid being impressed by some of these differences. Some people move quickly with explosive energy, some stroll languidly, some seem to fight a perpetual headwind. A teacher can quickly recognize the natural dynamics of her students and then encourage them to break away from their comfortable movement patterns to add variety and excitement. The monochromatic room mentioned earlier needs a persimmon or turquoise chair and vase; the bland untextured meal needs a tomato or crisp carrots! The slow-moving student needs to be told to stop and start suddenly, to jump or leap or quickly change direction.

Chapter Five

Elements of Choreography

Doris Humphrey, one of the greatest modern dance choreographers, has said choreography is the "art of making dances." Choreography includes the selection of movement appropriate to the meaning of the dance, the arrangement of movement in space with the group available, the over-all design of the dance and its staging. A choreographer must understand movement, music, and theater arts. From the very first pattern performed by dance students, elements of choreography are being emphasized, learned, and demonstrated.

Since dance is an art, all of the elements of art design apply also to dance design. The inter-relatedness of all the arts can be emphasized by examples drawn from other art fields. Some of the elements of over-all design applicable to choreography include symmetry and asymmetry, succession and opposition, line, shape, color, repetition and contrast, variety and unity, balance, perspective, style, and focal point of interest.

Beauty may "exist in the eye of the beholder" but a knowledge of the generally accepted conception of beauty may assist choreographers in achieving beautiful dances. Beauty requires integrity, proportion, and splendor:

Integrity: a well-knit internal unity or logic

Proportion: orderly arrangement of parts or sequence

Splendor: capacity for manifesting its pattern or harmony

In creating a work you have to have unity—but not so much unity it becomes boring; you have to have variety—but not so much it becomes chaos; then somewhere you have to have a climax. Effective choreography makes knowledgeable use of these elements of beautiful design so that the whole is greater than the sum of the individual parts. Esthetic principles are used to determine how the material (movement) is molded into a work of art (the completed dance).

The following elaboration on four elements of design shows briefly how they may be taught in specific relationship to dance.

Fig. 12-15. Symmetrical succession, symmetrical opposition, asymmetrical succession, asymmetrical opposition.

SYMMETRY

Symmetry refers to evenly-bàlanced design; the movement or position of one body in space or the movements and positions of several bodies in space. Symmetrical design, of course, is not limited to dance: architecture, furniture, and automobiles are usually symmetrical in design. The qualities communicated by evenly-balanced design are peace, harmony, calm, and completion. In dance, continual use of symmetry may cause a dance to be predictable and even boring.

ASYMMETRY

Asymmetry is unevenly-balanced design (the term unbalanced is not used for obvious reasons). A large group or a large movement may be balanced or complemented by a small group or a series of small movements. An artistic photograph or painting does not have the central focus of interest in the exact center of the composition: therefore its design is asymmetrical rather than symmetrical for maximum interest and effect. The qualities produced by asymmetry are power, excitement, interest, and surprise. However, continual use of extreme asymmetry may lead to confusion, disorganization, or even fatigue (on the part of the audience).

SUCCESSION

Succession in dance design refers to curved lines—in floor pattern and body design. The combination of succession and symmetry produces the most soothing and peaceful effect.

OPPOSITION

Opposition in design refers to straight and angular lines in movement or other design. Asymmetrical opposition provides the most powerful and exciting effect.

The way in which all these elements of design are used will depend upon the overall effect which the dancers wish to communicate. Needless to say, many other factors of design may be combined and emphasized in different ways in different parts of the same dance.

Generally, beginning dance students will choose to use symmetrical design: four slides right, four slides left; or a side-push to the right side, repeating the same movement to the left. Since techniques are practiced equally on each side, the students begin to think all movements must be repeated to each side. The instructor may need to emphasize the artistic interest of asymmetrical design, in individual movements and also in use of groups.

Two dancers who are performing the same movements (locomotor or axial) will strengthen the movement and the design if they move in unison, rather than in opposite directions. Adding more dancers moving in unison will multiply the power and effectiveness of even the simplest movement. This concept is quite different from formal classical ballet design which is usually evenly balanced to be "pretty." In modern dance a group of five dancers will probably be divided into two groups of 3 and 2 (● ● ●   ● ●) while in ballet a 2--1--2 (● ●   ●   ● ●) design is more apt to occur.

Students frequently need to have the obvious pointed out to them; their response is apt to be—"oh, of course, why didn't I think of that?" One such obvious factor of design (and choreography) is that some movements can be seen best by an audience if the dancers face downstage or upstage. Other movements have the greatest impact if the dancers are facing R stage or L stage (see illustration on p. 147). Having students perform a variety of movements facing in different directions, while others in the class watch, will help clarify this aspect of planning a dance.

PART TWO

Creative Approaches

Chapter Six
Use of Locomotor Movement

As defined previously, locomotor movement is movement through space, over a moving base. The best known and most widely used locomotor movement is a walk—a transfer of weight from one foot to the other, with at least one foot in contact with the floor at all times. One good starting point for a dance class is with an ordinary pedestrian walk—the way that the students usually walk around the school.

THE BASIC WALK

The pedestrian walk can be varied before it becomes a dance walk. Ask the students such questions as: how do you walk when you are in a hurry (change of tempo or rate of speed)? how do you walk on a lovely spring day (change of tempo and perhaps body position)? how do you walk when you are trying to sneak up on some one to surprise him? how do you walk through water or mud or snow? how do you walk when you are tired? or when you are carrying a heavy load?

Having the students experience each of these variations on a simple pedestrian walk can lead into establishing a dance walk: body extended, toes leading each step, weight transferring over a flexed knee, arms controlled rather than swinging freely. You may need to explain that, "If I saw you walking around school using this dance walk, I'd think it was pretty freaky too—but this is a dance class and even though we may start with natural movements you already know, we will always change or vary them when we use them as dance movements."

The use of the term "distortion" may be included here. It is important that students realize that distortion means *any* exaggeration or change from the natural or usual. Distortion does not mean an ugly change from the natural, even though that is the way many interpret the word.

Such a comment can lead directly into an exercise on inventing and demonstrating ways of varying a simple walk:

Directional changes: backward, sideward, turning, and circles.
Tempo changes: fast, slow, changing from fast to slow, alternating fast and slow.
Level changes: everything from tip-toes, with arms overhead as the highest level to a "duck" walk with deeply flexed knees as the lowest level.
Arm positions: for example, held akimbo, swinging freely, moving rhythmically at shoulder level, or tightly folded.
The legs: may be used in different ways (a kick and step, with a flexed knee or a straight knee, for example).
The body: may be upright or in a rounded position, twisted to one side or tilted to the side.
The steps: may be large or very small (variations in range).

Fig. 16.   Walk with variations.

The possibilities of varying a simple walk are practically endless. Starting with known material and then varying it is the basis for developing creative abilities in any field. In dance, teacher and student alike have a tremendous head start, since everyone has a body and everyone in a class can walk, bend and stretch, reach and pull, twist and turn, sit and rise. Learning to vary a *walk* provides the pattern for learning to vary other kinds of movement, using the same principles of space and time.

CREATIVE WALK PATTERNS

By demonstrating the following or posing the ideas as student problems, you can lead the student to use walk variations as the basis for a simple creative pattern.

1. *Walk, using a dance walk,* freely around the room, using all of the space available. Change direction sharply each time student meets another dancer directly or meets an obstacle (wall, equipment, door). Purpose: to realize the extent of space available.

2. *Change direction* on each measure of $\frac{4}{4}$ meter. Directional changes may be in terms of body direction or in terms of stage direction. Emphasis should be on clear direction of movement and sharp, exact changes of direction.

3. *With partner,* devise a pattern of 4 or 8 measures of moderate $\frac{4}{4}$ meter. The problem may be further defined: use a set number of different directions. Use a set number of measures in unison and a set number of measures in contrast.

Or start together (unison) and end together and in-between move in contrast. (Without mentioning form at this point, students will begin to feel the completeness of a pattern that has a definite beginning and ending.)

4. *Combine 2 or 3 sets* of partners into groups of 4 or 6. All will learn the previously set patterns and perform them in sequence to make a longer form.

5. *Perform in the groups* of 4 or 6 for the rest of the class.

6. *Whole class* may learn one of these longer sequences and perform it.

(The values of introducing large group performance at this early stage are: emphasis on group movement, rather than individual; realization of the increased strength and clarity of movement when multiplied by increased performers; loss of self-consciousness through group presentation; feeling of accomplishment in creative effort of *group;* awareness of roles of performers and audience.)

Continuing with the walk pattern, the students may be encouraged to add variations in level, style, arm movement, tempo, or rhythmic pattern. Several weeks could be spent on walks alone, with appropriate time allocated to technical development. Many elements of choreography can be emphasized in this elementary creative problem, as already indicated. A whole dance can be developed using only walk variations, but it may be preferable to add variety of creative stimuli by use of other locomotor movements.

OTHER LOCOMOTOR MOVEMENTS

Here are some suggestions for studies using other locomotor movements as the creative base.

1. *Practice other locomotor movements:* run, leap, jump, skip, hop, slide. Students should clearly differentiate between the different movements (see definitions in Part One) and be encouraged to avoid such definitions as: "a hop is a jump on one foot." Practice can be in mass formation or diagonally from one corner of room, moving in groups of 4 in sequence, or 4 groups from 4 corners of room.

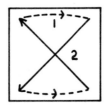 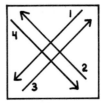

The choice will be determined by size of space available, size of group, and movement being practiced.

2. *Combine locomotor movements into patterns:*

    a. 4 runs, 4 slides, 4 skips, 4 jumps.
    b. 4 jumps, 4 hops, 4 jumps, 4 hops.
    c. 3 slides and 1 jump, 3 runs and 1 hop, run hop, run hop, 3 slides and 1 jump.
    d. any other combinations.

3. *Give class 3 measures* of locomotor patterns, each group to add a 4th measure.
4. *Give class 4 measures* of locomotor patterns, each group to add 4 more measures.
5. *Set limits and requirements for longer original pattern:* 8 measures, using at least 3 different locomotor movements and 3 different directions.

COMBINATION PROBLEM

Combining the walk pattern with pattern of other locomotor movements, assign a three-part problem in A-B-A form:

    (A) 1 phrase of walk
    (B) 1 phrase of other locomotion
    (A) 1 phrase of walk (repeat 1st phrase)

or

(A) 1 phrase of other locomotion
(B) 1 phrase of walk
(A) 1 phrase of other locomotion (repeat 1st phrase)

The foregoing study or pattern when thoroughly understood and carried out will give the students experience in sequential form—3 part song form (A-B-A) using familiar material. It will also help them learn how to use and mold material to achieve a longer pattern.

FINAL PROBLEM

Add a style or quality to the locomotor patterns, each group to choose its own style and method of achieving it. Some suggestions: Folk Dance, Western Square Dance, Jazz, Children's Game, March, Processional.

Chapter Seven
Use of Axial Movement

Just as each locomotor movement may serve as the basis for a creative problem, so each category of axial movement may also be used in similar fashion.

Work on swings should begin with some simple explanations and illustrations of a swing, a two-beat swing, and how to change levels while using swings. Note that the appropriate beat or music for accompaniment—at least at the beginning—is a slow ⅜ or ¾.

1. *The students should learn* and practice two-beat swings at all levels. A two-beat swing may be illustrated with this diagram:

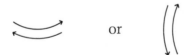

Emphasis should be on the curved line of movement, rebound to provide the second impetus, flexion and extension of knees on both halves of the two beats. A few examples of two-beat swings follow:

a. Standing:
From extended position, swing down, and then up again, (down and up and); from side to side—using body and then adding use of one arm and then both arms. The sideward swing may be started as a swaying movement and gradually increase in dimension to a fully extended swing, adding a lift of non-supporting leg at the end of each half of the two-beat swing.

b. Kneeling:

(1) Kneel-stand—swing down to kneel-sit and up. Rebound in knees should be emphasized.

(2) Kneel-sit—down-and-up swing; forward-and-back swing (extending to one hand support position); side-to-side (extending to one-hand support position at each side).

c. Sitting:

(1) Hurdle-sit—side-to-side swing, increasing dimension of swing to full extension in one-knee, one-hand support.
(2) One useful sequence—three swings to one side, each increasing in dimension. The beats for the fourth swing are used to change to opposite hurdle-sit.
(3) Rhythm— ♩ ♪ ♩ ♪ | ♩ ♪ ♩ ♪ |
Meter ⁶⁄₈: Swing out and back, and swing and swing and

♩ ♪ ♩ ♪ | ♩. ♩. |
Swing and swing and change sides

d. Lying Position:

(1) Back lying—swing up to sit and back to lying. Same swing on diagonal R and L.
(2) Side lying—leg swing: forward and back. Leg and arm swing, using either same direction or opposite direction for arm and leg.

2. *Improvisation.* Improvise on a two-beat swing at each level. Emphasis should be placed on trying to devise a swing which is different from those already learned and practiced. Unusual and interesting swings at each level can be selected, demonstrated, and learned by the whole class.

a. In three's—each group select a swing and teach it to the class. This can be done at each level.
b. Each student use all four levels—any starting position at each level: one swing at each level, repeated three times and using time of fourth swing to move to next level.
c. In groups of three to five students, repeat same problem: use of four levels, one original swing at each level: each swing repeated three times, with time of fourth swing used to change levels. Emphasis should be placed on contrast within the group so that several levels are used at same time. Each group will then perform their completed pattern for the class. The class may select the most interesting swing from each level and combine these into a pattern. Or several selected patterns may be used in sequence to produce a longer form.
d. Add quality or idea to swinging movement—for example: a lullaby or bell-ringing.

3. *Composition.* The poem ''The Bells'' by Edgar Allan Poe, might be used as the

culminating activity for the study of swings. The use of a gong and bells with different tones might also set an accompaniment for a final problem in swings.

CREATIVE APPROACHES USING SUSTAINED MOVEMENT

In using sustained movement as a starting point for creative work, it is possible to draw upon many previous technical experiences of the class, such as body stretches in all directions used to create flexibility. The specific emphasis now in sustained movement will be to experiment with new experiences to extend the range of movement and to achieve the desired quality of movement.

Begin by going over previous explanations of related techniques. Then explain how sustained movement (p. 6) differs consciously from other kinds of movement. Practice techniques to achieve strength in slow movement. Note that slow, strong music, whether dirges (slow marches) or a slow waltz rhythm, lends itself well to this kind of movement.

The following outline will give some ways of experimenting and improvising in sustained movement.

1. *Standing*

    a. Use of arms (ballet "port de bras" or carrying the arms):

    > (1) Lift arms from side of body to overhead and down again. Same with arms in front of body. The lift should be slow and with great strength: to achieve this the student can concentrate on internal resistance to movement.
    > (2) Also work in partners, with one partner providing the resistance: placing her hands on arms of student doing the lifting and lowering of arms.

    b. Body movement:

    > (1) Practice as if lifting a great weight—emphasis placed on use of body and legs in addition to strength in arms.
    > (2) With partner, lift and carry a heavy weight and place it down on floor. These are not dance movements, but pantomimic movements based on real movement intended to develop a feeling for the desired quality.
    > (3) Explore the range of sustained movement possible in standing position, without moving feet.

2. *Changing Levels*

    a. Move from standing level to lying down level and up again, using as much time as possible to complete the movement. Each student will discover for herself the most efficient and graceful way to accomplish the level changes.

b. Change level again very slowly from highest to lowest, stopping at each level (standing, kneeling, sitting, lying) to explore sustained body and arm movement at each level. Allow 16 or 32 slow counts to complete the sequence. Emphasis should be on continuity—a single sequence of strong, continuous movement from beginning to end.

3. *Experimentation in following movement*

a. Echo:

(1) Instructor stands (or kneels or sits) with back to class and moves 4 or 6 counts while class watches. Class echoes her movement, while leader rests. Changes of level can be included as well as sustained movement involving all parts of body. Leader should avoid turning since class will not be able to see the movement.
(2) Students in class lead the movement. If they hesitate to lead, a helpful approach may be to give the student an interesting starting position and have her move from there. Emphasis should be placed on spontaneous movement—not planning ahead.
(3) In partners—one serves as leader, the other repeats the movement while leader stops.

b. Mirror:

(1) Instructor faces class to lead the movement using the same pattern of moving and then holding the position while class moves. Class mirrors the movement: if leader uses R arm, class should use L arm. (This is a basic teaching method: if the teacher is facing the class, she will demonstrate with R arm while instructing class to use L arm.)
(2) With partners facing, one leads, the other mirrors the movement while the leader holds her position.
(3) With partners facing, mirror movement continuously. Students are always surprised and delighted that they can follow each other's lead without knowing in advance what the partner is going to do.

Fig. 17-18. Students mirror movements of the instructor.

c. Moving sculpture:

(1) Partners start facing each other. One starts the movement, the other moves in relationship to her partner's movement. For example: if A pushes toward B, B may move away. Movement continues with each being affected by the movement of the other.
(2) In three's, use the same exercise as above. Some interesting patterns may result so that it is helpful to have one-half of class watch the other half.
(3) In three's, students hold hands in circle of three and close eyes. The push-and-pull of sustained movement and its effect on others is exaggerated through the holding of hands. Emphasis should be placed on slow and continuous movement with response to the movement of the others in the circle to produce a piece of "moving sculpture."

Fig. 19.   Moving sculpture: the movement of each dancer is affected by that of her partner.

4. *Composition*

a. A short study in groups of three to five, using three levels, with contrast and unison, all movement to be continuous.
b. In groups of three to five, select a mood (for example, sorrow or peace) which can be portrayed through sustained movement.

c. Select a short musical composition which sets a mood for strong sustained movement. Some examples:

Satie's *Trois Gymnopédies* (particularly #3)
Hymns or religious songs
Beethoven's *Hymn to Joy*
Silent Night (at the proper season)
(Sometimes recordings of the themes from whatever movies are popular at the moment make the best stimulus for this kind of composition.)

CREATIVE USE OF PERCUSSIVE MOVEMENT

Experimentation in percussive movement may be developed as a study in itself or may be preparation for other creative problems, such as Primitive or Jazz. To give students the chance to experience the distinctive quality of percussive movement in various parts of the body is the aim of this section.

Discuss the percussion instruments: wood blocks, drums, cymbals, even piano (in Chapter Nine see p. 60 for a full explanation of this). Repeat the earlier descriptions of percussive movement and discuss the way in which drumbeats and strongly rhythmic music are best fitted to accompany percussive-type dances. Go over any techniques already learned which involve percussive movement.

1. *Locomotor movement with percussive accent*

    a. Walk variations

        (1) Toe-heel walk, accent on heel beat. Emphasis on using flexed knees.
        (2) Toe-heel, toe-heel, toe-heel, heel, heel. Practice forward and sideward. Add improvised percussive accent with arms or body, on heel beat.
        (3) Moving sideward—step R, step L across R, step R, jump in place. Improvise different percussive accents on count 4. Use the pattern: step, cross, step, accent as a 3-step turn and then a percussive movement on count 4. Use a sound with percussive accents: clap or slap on the leg, for example.

    b. Combination of locomotor movements
    Combine patterns of locomotor movements with percussive accent of body or feet. (Hops, jumps, leaps.)

        (1) Step hop, step hop, step, hop, hop, hop, jump (use 4 counts for the jump with body thrust up or body contraction).
        (2) Jump with body thrust up, contract, and twist after landing.
        (3) Step hop with body extended, free leg raised in back. Step hop with body contracted, free leg raised in front.

2. *Body movement with percussive beat*

   a. Hurdle-sit

      (1) Contract and extend (the simplest form of contraction is pulling in the center of body, bringing ribcage and hips closer together; extend is returning to upright position). Body can move directly forward or twist to either side on contraction. Position of arms and head may be varied.

      (2) Bounce and extend—body bounces forward or over either leg: 3 beats down for bounces and 1 beat up for extend.

      Teacher can give class one or two measures of beat, beat, beat, and up (meaning 3 bounces and a sharp extension) and then have class improvise variations on this pattern.

      All movement should be sharp and clear, in keeping with definition of percussive movement.

   b. Kneeling position

      (1) Kneel-sit (use same pattern as in hurdle-sit): beat, beat, beat, extend. On the beat, body will be rounded. On the extend, the body will thrust to a kneel stand or back extension.

      (2) Improvise other beating and striking movements in other kneeling positions.

   c. Standing

      (1) In stride position, R leg forward. Repeat pattern of beat, beat, beat, extend. On beat L arm and shoulder twist downward toward R foot; on extend L arm and shoulder are thrown up and back as body extends and twists L. Repeat with L arm; then on first beat, change feet with a jump.

      (2) Standing, feet together: step forward on R as body contracts forward; step R back to place as body returns to upright position.

      (3) Improvise striking, beating, and thrusting movements in a regular beat, using one or both arms and body in various directions and at various levels.

3. *Percussive patterns (creative)*

   a. With partner, compose a pattern of percussive striking movements, based on an idea such as: chopping wood; a boxing match; a series of karate strikes; pounding a fence post or tent pole.

   b. In a small group, compose a 4-measure phrase combining locomotor movement with percussive accents and percussive body movement without locomotion.

   c. In small groups, compose a 16-measure phrase, using 4 measures at each of at least 3 different levels, level changes to be made with percussive movement also.

4. *Composition—Culminating Activity:*

>a. Use percussion instruments (drums, cymbals, wood blocks) to provide the rhythmic pattern and accompaniment for percussive movement.
>b. Use authentic African, Cuban, or Haitian drum rhythms.
>c. In groups of three to five, select a mood (for example, excitement) which can be portrayed through percussive movement.
>d. Develop a primitive dance (see Chapter Thirteen) which is based on percussive movement (the primitive dance tends to be percussive since the dancers made their own accompaniment and kept time by body beats, heel beats, stamps, claps, and the like).

Percussive movement is more limited in its possible applications to choreography. There are only a few kinds of dances in which you would use mainly percussive movement. The majority of dances will use more sustained movement with percussive movement added as contrast. A whole dance of percussive movement is somewhat like hearing a jazz piece consisting entirely of a drum solo. Still it is important that students experience percussive movement and learn to use it creatively.

Chapter Eight
Creative Use of Space Elements

The human body is three-dimensional and even when motionless occupies space. The teacher and students need to be aware of how movement affects the space in which it exists and how the space affects the movement. A direct forward movement in the center of a stage has a different effect than a backward movement in the same area. A forward movement away from the audience is different from a forward movement toward the audience. A little experimentation, or demonstration by part of the class for the rest of the class, will make these space effects apparent.[1]

The two simplest aspects of the use of space—*direction and level*—have been rather fully discussed in the section on walks and the section on swings. A slight change of emphasis, directing the students' attention specifically to the space elements, would suffice to use either of these approaches.

FLOOR PATTERN
(USE OF DIRECTION)

For example, in a locomotor pattern, the concentration might be on developing a floor pattern which can be drawn on the chalkboard or on paper: for example,

Phrase 1   ⟶

(movement toward left stage)

---

[1]For a fine exposition of the space entity see Humphrey, Doris, *The Art of Making Dances.* N.Y., Rinehart & Winston, 1959. pp. 72-90. © 1959 by Charles F. Woodford and Barbara Pollack, edited by Barbara Pollack, Grove Press, Inc., N.Y., Evergreen Book.

Phrase 2

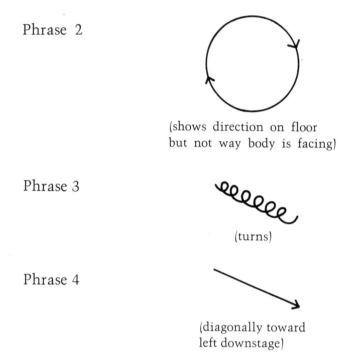

(shows direction on floor
but not way body is facing)

Phrase 3

(turns)

Phrase 4

(diagonally toward
left downstage)

The movements selected to achieve the pattern would be secondary, in this case, to the fulfilling of the problem: the primary emphasis would be on the accurate floor pattern drawn by the dancer's feet on the floor.

Floor patterns can be drawn for individuals, for partners, and for groups. The patterns can be simple as in the above examples, or complex, but should be clearly defined in the dancers' minds.

AMPLITUDE

Amplitude (or range) refers to the size of movement in space. The term is more often applied to axial movement than to locomotor movement but should not be limited to body movement. A walk may be small (on the toes, with straight legs) or large (a big stride from the hips, with flexed knees). A jump may be small and close to the floor or large, pushing off high from the floor or covering a wide area from take-off to landing.

The concept can be emphasized in many ways, a few of which are included here:

1. *Explain and demonstrate* the meaning of the term "range" with a simple arm movement, such as a sideward lift, from the shoulder, back of hand leading the movement.
2. *Increase size of movement* by continuing movement to shoulder level.
3. *Have class practice the smallest* such movement and the largest.

4. *Have class practice repeating* the movement, gradually increasing the size from largest to smallest.

5. *With partners*—contrast large, slow movement, with small, quick repetitions of movement—perhaps setting up a rhythm of 4 slow counts and 8 fast counts (1-2-3-4, 1&2&3&4&) performed simultaneously.

6. *Experiment with other movements,* both locomotor and axial, to determine extremes of range and contrasts of range.

7. *Use groups to emphasize* contrasts of range: large groups—large, slow movement; small group—small, fast movement; and then reverse.

8. *Provide opportunity* for students to watch each other in order to see as well as feel the range of movement. One-half of the class can perform and the other half watch or one group at a time can show the results of their experimentation.

CONTOUR

Contour means the outline of a figure in relation to the space around it. The figure need not be a body: buildings have contour, as do trees. A city skyline, silhouetted against a sunset, has a thrilling contour. The idea of a silhouette is perhaps the easiest for students to grasp in understanding the concept of contour. As related to dance, contour means the shape a dancer (or a group) assumes in relation to space.

Fig. 20. High and low shapes.

Attention to contour or body shape can lead to wide experimentation by the students in body position and movement. Frequently, an unusual starting position will lead to unusual movement while a usual or trite starting position may be followed by familiar or trite movement sequences.

Several approaches to contour are suggested in the following outline:

1. *Individuals assume a low body shape;* encourage unusual positions by selecting from class suggestions and having all the students try the selected "shape."

2. *Repeat with high body shape.* Point out that a high body shape does not have to be in the standing position and a low body shape does not have to be in a lying or sitting position. Low shapes will be mostly contracted. High body shapes will be mostly extended.

Fig. 21.   Demonstrates that a high shape need not be at a high level.

3. *Move from a low to a high shape* and vice versa quickly, as on the sudden beat of a drum. The beat can be at irregular intervals to make the students' response percussive in nature.

4. *Move slowly from a low to a high shape,* and vice versa, emphasizing the transitional movement as well as the low and high shapes.

5. *Draw a contour or silhouette* on the board and have groups reproduce the contour in body position. For example:

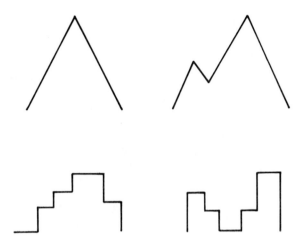

Symmetrical and asymmetrical design can be emphasized and demonstrated.

6. *Have groups move quickly* from one contour to another on beat of drum.

7. *Have groups move slowly* from one contour to another, holding each contour for a set number of beats before moving to the next.

8. *Discuss relationship of contour* to emotional quality: low contour of group to indicate sorrow, high contour to indicate joy. Or low contour to indicate slavery, high contour to indicate freedom. Have each group select two contrasting feeling states or two contrasting ideas and develop contours for each. This approach is one way for a group to start creating a dance: to select a group contour or starting position which clearly indicates the feeling or idea which they wish to express and then to develop movement from that group shape in space.

FOCUS

Focus means the central point of interest; many times in dance, this refers to the direction of the gaze but it may also refer to the direction of attention as indicated by the attitude of the body. Too often beginning dancers develop bad habits of focus: looking downward at the floor as a reflection of self-conciousness or embarrassment. The instructor should encourage the students to use focus as an integral part of the movement to emphasize its direction and its impact.

1. *In practicing locomotor movement,* the focus is usually straight ahead, but the focus can be directed in other ways to change the quality of movement. For example, in a walk pattern, moving diagonally from corner to corner of the room:

> 4 walks with focus straight ahead
> 4 walks with focus downward
> 4 walks with focus on the ceiling
> 4 walks with focus behind (more of the body moves here)
> 4 walks with shifting focus on each step from R to L side

In order for the changes of focus to be effective, the head should move as well as the eyes, so that the face is turned in the same direction as the eyes. As the students watch each other performing this simple pattern, they will become more conscious of the relationship of focus and movement.

2. *Another short exercise* in focus can involve fixing the gaze on a spot on the wall or ceiling: a specific light fixture or ventilation grill perhaps. Instruct students to move as if they are terrified by the "spot" and to move slowly and fearfully away from it. Or to move as if they are irresistibly drawn to the spot. Intensity can be added if the eyes never leave the focus spot, regardless of the movement of body or legs. The concentration of the eyes of a group on a single spot will give unity to even improvised movement. Or practice other ways of communicating that the spot is the center of attention. Half of the class should watch this improvisation by the other half of the class to realize the full effect of concentration.

Fig. 22.   Focus can be used to intensify emotional impact.

3. *One other study in focus* merits a brief discussion—the effect of shifting focus. If a feeling of indecision, uncertainty, or confusion is desired, a rapidly shifting focus may achieve the desired result. In any selected starting position, students will remain motionless, while rapidly shifting the focus of the head and eyes in many directions. Repeat in another starting position, moving the eyes and the head in continuous sharp changes of focus. A third step in the study would be to add locomotor movement forward, backward, or in circles to the rapid change of focus. Allow students to see the differences in meaning which occur with change of tempo and change of focus—slow movement with slow change of focus (searching), slow movement with rapid change of focus (fear), rapid change of focus with rapid movement (indecision).

Here are two additional studies on a more advanced level in which the starting point for creative work is a factor of space. Both of these set limitations on space, real or imaginary, and both can lead to full-fledged dances if the original improvised study is expanded and set in a form for performance.

REAL LIMITS ON SPACE

The real limits on space for these problems are achieved by the use of stage sets or properties. What happens to your space when you throw something into the middle of it? It changes your movements—a fact that students need to experience. The students may select their own or may be assigned particular space-limiting objects.

1. *In a gymnasium,* objects such as a balance beam, a stack of mats, or a group of volleyball standards, a table, or one or more chairs are frequently already available.
2. *Other objects* such as portable screens, saw-horses, a cage ball, a nylon parachute, a heavy velvet drape, or a number of hula-hoops might be brought into the class by the instructor or the students. Each object or group of objects will in some way affect the space available for the group to move in. This is the object of the study: to clearly delineate how movement in space is affected by objects which limit the space.
3. *Examples of how some classes* have solved this problem:

> a. In one dance, using six volleyball standards, the group constructed an enclosed space by setting the poles in a circle. This enclosed space became a prison with some dancers trying to break out, others trying to break in. The tension created was a palpable entity, the direct result of the use of space-limiting objects.
> b. Another dance used a large cage-ball in a playful way—arms, legs, and heads appeared and disappeared around the ball which ended up being a large snowball gathering dancers as it rolled off the stage. Dancers and audience alike had fun with this dance,

proving once again that dance does not have to be serious to be effective.

c. A third group used two saw-horses as its space-limiting objects. To the music of Gershwin's "Summertime," the dancers languidly stretched on and circled over the objects, moving them as a part of the dance to form new levels, shapes, and contours.

IMAGINARY SPATIAL LIMITS

There is another way of enhancing students' awareness of space: the creation of imaginary spatial limits. How would you move in a tunnel? in a box? on a high, narrow ledge? What effect would a wall have on your movement? How can you show wide open, unrestricted space? The crucial point of these studies is that each group has the spatial restriction so clearly in mind that the audience will also "see" the exact location and dimension of the limited space. Direct pantomime should be avoided—but derived pantomime may be helpful. For example, in defining the limits of a box, patting the hands along a side and a top of a cube might be considered real pantomime, while the same movements set into a rhythmic pattern and a repeatable sequence might be considered derived pantomime.

1. *Preliminary work.* In stimulating groups to use their imagination to fulfill this problem, have them answer questions like:

> Where is the structure on the floor?
> How large is it? how high? how long? how wide?
> What position will make it clear to the audience? (Regarding a tunnel, for example, should it point to the audience or be parallel to it?)
> What is the feeling you get when you think about being in a box or a tunnel or on a high, narrow ledge?
> What kind of movement, what body positions will best clarify your problem to an audience?

The instructor can use these general questions with the whole class in preparing for the study and then be more specific as she moves around to assist each group.

For a "wall" group, the following questions might be appropriate:

> Is it a high wall or a low wall?
> Is it situated from upstage to downstage or from right to left or is it on a diagonal?

Can you go around the ends of it or does it block the whole area?
Are you going to plan to conquer the wall or be frustrated by it?
What happens if you run and are stopped by a wall?
What different ways can you use to get over a wall?

Similar series of questions can be used with each group to stimulate their thinking about their own specific space limitations. A problem which has the purpose of communicating a specific idea often triggers highly imaginative responses without the trauma produced by a large, vague idea. (Students may want to dance about conflict or democracy or peace but they will have difficulty in communicating these ideas to an audience.) Here again is a demonstration of the step-by-step method of learning to be creative and communicative.

2. *Performance.* The imaginary limitations on space problem has been successfully used in several ways.

a. One way is to permit students to set up their own groups, select their own space limitations (or in contrast, a lack of limitation: wide open space), to create their dance and then present it to the rest of the class. The class should be able to determine what the group is representing without being told.
b. The class may also be divided into groups by any of several different methods (see Part Three) and then assigned a specific problem to work on. In this way, the instructor will be sure that each of the examples will be represented. Free choice may result in seven walls and no tunnel, box, or ledge!
c. The class may also be asked to suggest other imaginary limits of space and, if these are easily definable, they can well be substituted or added to the list suggested by the instructor.
d. If a demonstration or performance is planned to illustrate many different approaches to dance composition, several of the space limitation dances might be good to include in finished form. Electronic music or other music without strict melody or form provides excellent background accompaniment. One group used words spoken by the dancers as accompaniment to illustrate wide open space. The words were *down, up, out,* and *around,* repeated in different rhythmic patterns, at various pitches with different intonations and at contrasting tempos to emphasize the movement.
e. Another use for this study is in a class or even a master class when a short improvisational creative work is desired. If an instructor wants to include creative work as part of a final examination for a dance class, she may select this approach to creative work. Within fifteen minutes, most groups can create and be ready to perform a short study to illustrate one of these imaginary space limitations.

f. Similarly, in a master class or dance symposium where students from different schools or different classes are working together, this problem has been successfully used. Dissimilarities in technical experience or background seem to be unimportant when working on this kind of creative problem. The students usually enjoy it and can complete it successfully in a comparatively short time.

Chapter Nine
Using Time Elements Creatively

Training and experience in the use of time elements in dance begin with the first dance class and continue during the entire dance experience. The response to meter or underlying beat, to musical phrases, and to varying tempos is an integral part of every dance experience, whether or not it is directly emphasized by the instructor. For example, students quickly absorb the fact that in dance, most techniques or patterns are built in a series of four or eight rather than multiples of ten as in calisthenics or gymnastic exercise. Musical form is constructed in this way and since music is the most common dance accompaniment, dance is also so structured. Techniques are used, then, not only for movement experience and physical discipline but also for rhythmic training.

Some aspects of time lend themselves specifically to creative manipulation, providing both intellectual understanding of rhythmic principles and stimulus for creative work. A few of these will be discussed in this section.

RHYTHMIC PATTERNS

The combinations of short and long beats superimposed on a basic meter can be used in a number of different ways.

For rhythmic training: a rhythmic pattern can be played on the dance drum and reproduced in locomotor movement by the class.

1. *Leader plays* a rhythmic pattern for one measure of four counts. Example:

♩ ♫ ♩ ♩ |

Class reproduces the pattern with the feet, moving in a large circle. Repeat, for a number of different patterns.

2. *Leader alternates* one measure of four quarter notes with one measure of varied rhythmic pattern. Example:

$$\left.\sdownarrow \sdownarrow \downarrow \downarrow \right| \downarrow \musicnote \musicnote \downarrow \left| \downarrow \downarrow \downarrow \downarrow \right| \musicnote \downarrow \musicnote \downarrow \right|$$

Class starts moving one measure after the leader starts the drum beats, so that when they are walking the quarter notes, they are listening to the next rhythmic variation.

IMPROVISATIONS ON RHYTHMIC PATTERNS

1. *Use same procedure* (alternating quarter notes with varied rhythmic patterns—adding a single improvised element, such as a change of direction on each measure of quarter notes or a change of level on the quarter notes or a body or arm movement on the quarter notes rather than a foot pattern. These experiences require intense concentration and provide excellent training in coordinating auditory and muscular responses.

2. *Name patterns*

    a. Select names of students in class and clap out the rhythmic pattern of the names. For example:

Jennifer Jones

Linda Lopez

Mary Lou Kennedy

    b. Each student will then clap out the pattern of her own name, checking with instructor for accuracy in determining meter and note pattern.

    c. Each student will then reproduce her own name rhythm in movement, perhaps first with the feet only and then using body or arm movements in addition to foot patterns.

    d. In groups of three or four, use the name patterns of each member of the group, making the presentation interesting in terms of choreography: use of group and solo movement, use of direction, use of varied kinds of movement, while still accurately following the rhythmic patterns.

    e. This device has possibilities for performance also: when introducing a group of dancers, name patterns might be used as the basis for introduction. Each dancer or the group could reproduce the rhythmic pattern of her name, in a style or movement sequence appropriate to the dancer. The possibilities inherent in such introductions are delightful (or monotonous) depending on the originality of timing, movement, and variations.

3. *Body rhythms.* Historically, the first accompaniment for movement consisted of body rhythms: claps, stamps, slaps, grunts, and other vocal sounds. This kind of accompaniment can be used in several ways.

a. In groups, students develop a rhythmic pattern for a given number of measures. The pattern should be clear enough in the students' minds so that it can be written on chalkboard or paper.

b. The rhythmic pattern is reproduced in body sounds, using more than one type of body sound—clap, slap, heel click and the like.

c. The rhythmic pattern is reproduced in movement, either locomotor or axial, accompanied by body sounds, as above. The group may choose to have all members move and accompany in unison or to divide the two types of patterns, with part of the group moving and part accompanying. If the latter method is chosen, the two roles may be exchanged during the sequence or remain the same throughout.

4. *Nursery rhymes or jingles.* The rhymes we learn in childhood are usually written in strongly rhythmed (as well as rhymed) verse and thus are easily converted into rhythmic patterns to be used for movement patterns.

a. Have each group select and perform a favorite childhood rhyme by marking the rhythm with body sounds and movements.

Example:
Jack and Jill went up the hill to fetch a pail of water

♩　♪　♩　♪ | ♩　♪　♩　♪ | ♩　♪　♩　♪ | ♩. ♩.

Both the rhythm and the meaning of the nursery rhyme in this case lend themselves to swinging, skipping, or sliding patterns.

b. One way to check the accuracy of each group's performance is to have the rest of the class guess what nursery rhyme or jingle has been selected, clap the rhythmic pattern as they say it, and then have the group perform again to the accompaniment of the rest of the class.

5. *Cheers or yells.* If a study in rhythmic patterns occurs during football or basketball season or if spirit leaders (song and cheer leaders) are in the dance class, school cheers may be analyzed for rhythmic patterns and reproduced in group movement. Example (two common football cheers):

We want a touch down

♩　♪　♪　♩　　♩ :‖

Hold that line

$^4_4$ 𝅘𝅥   𝅘𝅥   𝅘𝅥 :‖

Individual school cheers are apt to be more complicated but can provide an interesting challenge for the same kind of analysis.

PERCUSSION INSTRUMENTS

The study of rhythmic pattern and rhythm in general can be profitably combined with an examination of the use of percussion instruments. Just as the use of body rhythms provided the basis for a rhythmic study, so too can percussion instruments be used. Any instrument—including the piano—which produces sound through beating, shaking, or striking can be classified as percussion. Drums of all kinds, rattles, cymbals, gongs, sticks, maracas, and tambourines are some of the readily available percussion instruments. If none or few of these are available in the dance class, students may be able to bring some from home or the music department may have some. In fact, students can improvise such instruments with wooden spoons, shells, gourds, and boxes—a fine project for interdepartmental cooperation.

1. *Patterns.* Having selected one or more instruments, the students, in groups, next set up a clear rhythmic pattern for a given number of measures. These rhythmic patterns should always be written out in notes and measures (on blackboard or paper) and checked to make sure that the correct number of beats occur in each measure. Example:

$^4_4$ 𝅘𝅥𝅮𝅘𝅥𝅮𝅘𝅥𝅘𝅥𝅮𝅘𝅥𝅮𝅘𝅥𝅘𝅥 | 𝅘𝅥𝅘𝅥𝅘𝅥𝅮𝅘𝅥𝅮𝅘𝅥 |

Measure one correctly totals four beats while measure two is incomplete for a $^4_4$ meter. Parenthetically, measure two would be a complete measure for $^3_4$ meter: if the students plan to change meters, an added element of excitement may result. If they know what they are doing—fine.

2. *Patterns of movement.* After a clear and varied rhythmic pattern has been developed, the group will then devise movement to reproduce the pattern. Movement may be locomotor or axial; the original choice of instruments as well as the rhythmic pattern will determine the selection of movement. The development of this pattern may be *preceded* by an exploration of percussive movement (so that the movement is the starting point) or may be *followed* by movement exploration (so that the instruments are the stimulus). The two approaches may proceed simultaneously, with techniques and improvisation in percussive movement leading to creative work on a rhythmic base.

3. *Percussion accompaniment.* In presenting this dance pattern to the class, each group will have to decide how to use its selected instruments in accompaniment.

Several choices are obvious:

> Group moves and plays instruments simultaneously;
>
> Part of group dances, part accompanies;
>
> Group dances, another group accompanies, from written rhythmic pattern.

4. *Primitive dances from percussion approaches.* If high interest is generated by use of percussion instruments, an extended dance can be developed using a primitive theme. Both performers and audience usually find such dances to be program highlights. Further discussion of this approach will be found in Chapter Thirteen.

RESULTANT METERS

Resultant meters are achieved by combining the accented beats of two separate meters, used simultaneously (as shown in Part One, Chapter Three).

Preparatory work: before the students can use this rhythmic device creatively, they must have a clear understanding of how the resultant meter is achieved.
1. *Writing the pattern* on the board and then having the student clap and listen to the accents will probably help clarify the rhythmic structure. The simplest resultant combines a $\frac{2}{4}$ meter with a $\frac{3}{4}$ meter, giving a resultant meter of $\frac{6}{4}$ with one primary and three secondary accents—all of the accents taken from both meters.

$\frac{2}{4}$	1	2	1	2	1	2
$\frac{3}{4}$	1	2	3	1	2	3
$\frac{6}{4}$	1	2	3	4	5	6

2. *Class can be divided* in half and, reading from the board, one group claps the $\frac{2}{4}$ meter, one the $\frac{3}{4}$ meter, accenting the first beat of each measure. (A word of warning: help students maintain an even tempo.) Each half can clap their own meter separately first and then both together. As they listen to both meters performed simultaneously, they will begin to realize when both groups hit beat number one together (every six counts) and this will help them to understand the concept of a six-beat measure.
3. *The two groups can also* stand and face each other, stepping in place in their own meter: a down step (knee flexed) on accent and an up step (on toes) on unaccented beats.

When the students see and hear the resultant rhythm from simultaneous performance of the two original meters, they are ready to perform the resultant as a separate pattern.
4. *One clear form would be* (using claps) Group I—$\frac{2}{4}$ meter 6 measures, then Group II—$\frac{3}{4}$ meter 4 measures, then Group I and Group II—repeat same, together, then Group I and Group II—two measures of $\frac{6}{4}$ resultant. The same form could be repeated with the down and up steps in place if necessary to clarify the pattern.

5. *Creative use.*

   a. Rhythmic approach

      (1) In groups: each group select the two meters they want to combine and write out the resultant.

      (2) Put into form: number of measures of each meter and number of measures of resultant.

      (3) Determine sequence: for example, each meter separately first, then both meters together, then resultant (as in practice pattern). The reverse order could also be selected: resultant first, then both meters together, then each meter separately.

        A number of other sequences could be selected by various groups, so long as the form is clearly defined.

      (4) Select movements, either locomotor, axial, or combined which clearly define the two separate meters.

      (5) Select movement which combines the accented beats of the two separate movements to achieve a resultant movement following the accented beats of the resultant meter.

      (6) Perform for the rest of the class.

   b. Use of resultant to clarify an idea

      (1) Discuss with class how use of resultant could clarify an idea: two opposing groups or ideas, combining or compromising to reach a resolution.

      (2) Divide class into groups larger than usual, to fulfill this assignment.

      (3) Have each group select two opposing ideas and a resolution of them. Examples:

          Pioneers vs. Indians ▶ smoking peace pipe
          (symbolically of course)
          Sun vs. Rain ▶ Rainbow

      (4) Have each group select the two meters they wish to use, work out the resultant meter and structure the form of dance:

          Sequence of meters
          Number of measures of each
          Number of measures of resultant

      (5) If necessary, help each group create the movements to follow the chosen meters and to express the ideas selected.

      (6) Ask each group to perform for the rest of the class.

      (7) Evaluate, in conjunction with the class, based on clear use of resultant and expression of the idea, as well as on the usual aspects of good choreography.

ACCUMULATIVE METER AND DIMINISHING METER

Many techniques are taught and practiced in accumulative or diminishing meters (pliés and relevés, bounces and stretches, falls and recoveries) so the concept is not new when it is introduced as a springboard for creative work.

1. *Preliminary work*

 a. To review the terms: accumulative meter means increasing the number of beats per measure in a regular sequence:

$$\frac{1}{4}\ \mathrel{\vert}\ \frac{2}{4}\ \mathrel{\vert}\ \frac{3}{4}\ \mathrel{\vert}\ \frac{4}{4}\ \mathrel{\vert}\text{ and so on.}$$

Diminishing meter means decreasing the number of beats per measure in a regular sequence:

$$\frac{8}{4}\ \mathrel{\vert}\ \frac{4}{4}\ \mathrel{\vert}\ \frac{2}{4}\ \mathrel{\vert}\ \frac{1}{4}\ \mathrel{\vert}$$

Any other sequence is equally usable.

 b. Preliminary work may include practicing walks in accumulative and diminishing meter, changing direction on each measure. Walks can be forward and backward on alternate measures; a quarter- or half-turn can be used on count one of each succeeding measure; or combinations of forward, backward, and sideward walks, and quarter- and half-turns can be used. Emphasis should be placed on accuracy of changes and dance quality in the walks. Axial movements can also be used, improvisationally, to indicate these rhythmic changes: a percussive accent on beat one with follow-through on the remaining beats in each measure.

2. *Pattern*

 a. A structured assignment might be for each group to use one phrase in locomotor movement, one phrase in axial movement, and a last phrase in locomotor movement. The pattern could be written on the chalkboard in the following ways:

1				one phrase—to fulfill the above problem, this pat-
1	2			tern would be performed three times. If you write
1	2	3		this out on the board, explain that the numbers
1	2	3	4	denote the counts in each measure.
1	2	3		
1	2			
1				

An alternate method of writing the pattern:

$$\|\mathrel{:}\ \mathrel{\vert}\ \mathrel{\vert}\ \mathrel{\vert}\ \mathrel{\vert}\ \mathrel{\vert}\ \mathrel{:}\|$$

Repeat two more times.

 b. A drum provides the suitable accompaniment since the accented beats (number one of each measure) can be clearly defined. However, music with a definite $\frac{4}{4}$ meter provides an interesting alternative for this particular accumulative-diminishing pattern, since one phrase is equivalent to 4 measures of $\frac{4}{4}$ meter. (Add them up and see.)

3. Choreographic Uses

a. In addition to the abstract movement study based on accumulative meter, the pattern has been used successfully to achieve certain effects in choreography. In a prison-yard sequence, part of one long dance a group of students developed, the dancers paced back and forth in the accumulative-diminishing pattern, creating the feeling of monotony while still capturing the audience through the unpredictability of the pacing.

b. In a comic scene, a group of badly trained soldiers marched in seemingly haphazard fashion, alternating regular marching with marching in accumulative patterns. The effect was chaos, but the chaos was controlled, each "soldier" knowing his own pattern and all ending together, to the delighted applause of the audience.

c. Another group used the accumulative meter in a dance of the industrial age. To produce the effect of a machine, each dancer, or group of dancers, used one of the meters for her mechanical movement. The over-all effect was of machine parts moving in sequence, but there was no monotony because each part of the machine moved in a different meter.

d. Focusing directly on accumulative-diminishing meters as a starting point for creative work will help the students see the possibilities of using this rhythmic device in other ways to add interest and variety to dances which have a different creative base.

USE OF MUSIC

Years ago, music visualization was an important part of dance choreography: if the music went up the scale, the dancers moved upward, or perhaps each dancer followed the musical line of one specific instrument in an orchestral composition.

Dance was also used as "musical interpretation." The era of "natural dance," which was inspired by Isadora Duncan and her disciples, emphasized dance as an interpretation of music. Many musicians feel that it is presumptuous for one art form (dance) to claim to interpret another art form (music). Dancers and dance teachers agree that dance can stand on its own two feet (pun intentional!) as an art form. Concert or professional dancers often prefer to create a dance and then to have the musical accompaniment composed for the dance. While this is usually not possible in school situations, music can be used as accompaniment rather than as the sole stimulus for creative work.

The students can decide what kind of dance they wish to compose and then search to find a musical composition which has the appropriate quality, rather than selecting a piece of music and then composing a dance to it. One would not select a funeral march as accompaniment for a dance of joy!

Fig. 23-24. A musical selection about brotherhood produced a dance with strong emotional content.

Once the music is selected, the over-all structure of the music will help determine the form of the dance. The meter, phrase length, tempo, and form can appropriately be followed in the choreography. The dynamics and climaxes in the music can be reflected in the dance but each rise and fall of melodic line, each accent or volume change need not be slavishly followed.

Music can be used as background for a dance just as a stage set can be used to *add to* the dance without being a *part of* the dance. Electronic or improvisational music, which does not have a clearly defined form, is appropriate for use in this way.

An example from folk music will illustrate the above approach: a Negro spiritual "Git on Board Little Chillen." This selection might be chosen for a number of different reasons: as part of a suite of spirituals, as an example of musical form, as accompaniment for a dance based on locomotor movement, or a dance with a light, happy quality.

The meter is set: $\frac{4}{4}$.

The form is A, B (verse and chorus) repeated as often as desired.

The quality is lively and spirited.

The phrases are four measures in length. The tempo is moderately fast.

With this information, the dance can be composed without constantly listening to the music. The form of the dance will follow the form of the music but the composition will be focused on movement appropriate to the quality selected for the dance.

Previous emphasis in class on time elements (such as meter, tempo, phrases, and form) will help the students to analyze a musical composition which is being used for dance accompaniment.

Chapter Ten

Gesture

It has been said that creative work depends largely on the rearrangement of known materials. Certainly for beginning dance students this statement is usually true. Rarely do students produce entirely original movements, although some of the movements may seem to be original to the performers. Helping students find new ways to vary known movements is one way to increase creative effort and ability.

One large category of known movements lies in the field of *gesture*. A dictionary definition of "gesture" is "movement of hands, arms, or any part of the body, used instead of words, or with words, to help express an idea or feeling."

Ask a class what a gesture is and immediately there will be nods, shrugs, waving, the hitch-hiker's thumbing, beckoning

KINDS OF GESTURES

A discussion of the *kinds* of gestures can be directed toward the following classification:

1. *Social gestures:* waving, handshaking, nodding or shaking the head, beckoning, or pushing away.
2. *Functional gestures:* recognizable movements from everyday life such as sweeping, washing, bathing, hammering, chopping, boxing, shooting baskets.
3. *Emotional gestures:* crying, laughing, hugging, rejecting.
4. *Ritual gestures:* praying, saluting, curtseying, bowing.

Any of these types of gestures may be used as the basis for this particular study— but in selecting a gesture, the students should have clearly in mind the category and the familiarity of the gesture to others. Gestures vary with different cultures and different ethnic groups and those chosen should be easily recognizable and have a generally accepted meaning.

PANTOMIME

The second step is to expand the chosen gesture into a brief pantomime. In drama, a pantomime is a play without words, an expression through gestures. For our purposes in this particular study, a pantomime will be an exaggerated gesture, set in repeatable form.

1. *Range:* the exaggeration may be in terms of range to make the movement larger or smaller.
2. *Rhythm:* repetition of the movement in a set metrical or rhythmic pattern.
3. *Space:* add movement through space to a stationary gesture.
4. *Body involvement:* adding use of a different part of the body or an additional part of the body to the original gesture.

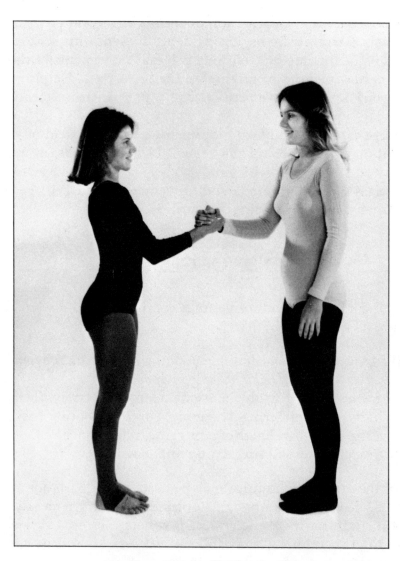

Fig. 25.   Gesture: Shaking hands.

DANCE

Following the development of the pantomime (which is an *exaggerated* gesture), the group will *abstract* the gesture into a dance. The *meaning* of the gesture (as well as the original movement of the gesture) will be the basis for the dance.

Example—the social gesture of *handshaking*.

Gesture: couples in group shake hands.

Pantomime: couples in group exaggerate the gesture, for instance:

Up and down movement of one leg and one arm, partners facing.

Small vibratory movement of hands up and down.

Rhythmic extension and withdrawal of alternate hands and arms toward partner.

Fig. 26.   Pantomime: an exaggeration of a handshake.

Dance: dance of meeting and greeting.
The same sequence can be followed in expanding any gesture into a dance.

Chopping	(into)	work dance
Crying	(into)	dance of sorrow
Beckoning	(into)	dance of flirtation
Waving goodbye	(into)	dance of parting

The intermediate stage of pantomime is included to simplify the expanding of a concrete gesture into abstract but meaningful dance.

PERFORMANCE

In performance, the original gesture can be demonstrated in unison, the pantomime performed in unison, or with partners or in groups, and the dance presented as a complete choreographic masterpiece.

Fig. 27. A dance of greeting.

Chapter Eleven
Feelings

Body language, the basis for much dance movement, is always used to express a person's feelings. The carriage of the body unconsciously communicates how one feels—"bowed down by sorrow," "frozen by fear," "strike out in anger" are common expressions reflecting the body language of emotions. If a teacher asks a class to show anger, she will see stamping feet, flailing fists, tension throughout the body. If she asks "how do you show sorrow," she will see bowed heads, rounded backs, hands or arms covering the face and head. "How do you show happiness or 'joie de vivre,'" will result in jumps, leaps, twirls, body and arms extended upward, faces lifted to the ceiling.

To reverse the process, give a class a rounded and bowed position and ask them how they feel. The answers will be sad, sorrowful, grieving. So body position and movement not only reflect inner feelings, they can also produce those same feelings.

Since the body, whether dancing or not, *does* communicate feelings, moods, and emotions, dancers should know *what* they are communicating and how to say, non-verbally, what they wish to say.

PRELIMINARY WORK

1. *Discuss with class* and list the "dark" emotions (hate, anger, fear) and the "light" emotions (love, joy, happiness).
2. *Discuss with class* and list varying degrees for one or two feelings (for example: happiness, joy, ecstasy; sorrow, grief, agony).
3. *Discuss with class* and list series of contrasting emotions (for example: love-hate, joy-grief, fear-courage, despair-hope).

PROCEDURE

The following outline will indicate some of the ways of transferring realistic body language into dance communication, in much the same way that gestures were abstracted into dance.

1. *Ask class to show anger* in body movement. If the first displays are too restrained, class can be encouraged to "throw a temper tantrum," to strike out, to kick, to throw something (imaginary) against a wall.

2. *Repeat* with several other feeling states:

  grief ("show me how you cry")

  fear ("How would you move to get away from a large, vicious animal?")

  happiness ("How do you move on a lovely spring day or on the last day of school?")

Fig. 28. The emotion of sorrow is expressed through the drawn-in tense position of body and head.

3. *Select one or two* of the feeling states, and have students start with the realistic body positions and movements expressive of this feeling. Then instruct the class to abstract the realistic movement into a dance phrase, with movements, dynamics, and rhythm which can be repeated.

4. *Divide class* in groups, each group to select a mood or feeling to express in dance. A helpful procedure is to have each group demonstrate an appropriate starting position before continuing into dance movement.

5. *When dances are completed* (to accompaniment selected by each group), the rest of the class can watch and "guess" the emotion or mood of each dance.

6. *For performance,* several groups can be combined to show the varying degrees of a single feeling (as indicated in preliminary discussion). For example: happiness, joy, ecstacy, or fear, panic, terror. The three groups in each case need not be separate but can instead choreograph the original three dances into a unified whole.

7. *Contrasting emotions* can also be choreographed into a single dance—a "dark" emotion and its contrasting "light" emotion. A single group may select the double assignment or two groups can be combined to illustrate the opposing emotions.

COLORS EVOKING FEELING RESPONSES

1. *Discuss with class* what each color means to them, in terms of emotion. Red-Anger, Purple-Passion, Yellow-Gaiety. Usually there are several words for each color, but the differences are a matter of degree rather than of kind.

2. *Divide class* in groups according to the color they wish to work on or let each group select its own color.

3. *The dances* will be created to express the emotional impact of the color, with all the usual aspects of good choreography being utilized. Since the creative problem involves two abstractions—color and feeling—advanced students (second semester or second year) will probably be more successful in achieving worthwhile results.

4. *For performance,* "A Rainbow of Colors" might be presented.

5. *Suggested records:*

       "Tone Poems in Color" (Capitol W735)

       "The Passions" (Capitol LAL 486)

Fig. 29. The emotion of joy is expressed through lift and elevation of entire body.

Chapter Twelve
Movement and Words

Words are sometimes used to explain dances but basically dance is direct communication without words. Words can, however, be used as a stimulus for creative work, whether in the form of poetry, stories, or ideas. In the same way that space elements, rhythmic elements, music, or gestures provide the impetus or springboard, so too can words be used.

When words are used as the starting point for a dance, they can also be incorporated into the dance in various ways. The simplest way is to have the poem or other words printed in the program or read before the dance is performed. This method uses the words to explain the dance but does not make the poem an integral part of dance.

A second plan is to have the words spoken at appropriate times during the dance, a word or a phrase at a time, to add meaning to a specific part of the movement. A third use would be for the dancers themselves to incorporate the words into the plan of the dance and to speak the words themselves, providing complete integration of words and movement.

EXAMPLES

Poems which have a definite rhythm—such as Vachel Lindsay's "Congo"—may be performed by a chanting or reciting choir providing the sole accompaniment for the dance. A cantata such as William Schuman's "A Free Song" may be sung and recited by a full choir with the dance following ideas of the words and the structure of the music. "A Jazz Fantasia" by Carl Sandburg involves both rhythms and ideas which can provide the basis for a group dance. These last three projects would be for advanced students but are cited as examples of the range of possibilities for the use of words and movement.

HAIKU POETRY

Haiku (pronounced hi-coo) poetry provides one excellent source for dance composition based on words. Haiku is an ancient form of Japanese poetry always written in seventeen syllables and three lines: the first and third lines with five syllables, the second line with seven syllables. Good translations from the Japanese capture the meaning of the poem and also retain the form: seventeen syllables in English (although this is not always possible).

Usually Haiku is written about some aspect of nature (a season, a plant, an animal) or about man in relationship to some aspect of nature. Frequently, "there is also an implied identity between two seemingly different things."[1] One can readily see that the short three line poem is provocative rather than exhaustive in its meanings. This is exactly why Haiku is such an interesting starting point for dance composition.

The poet expects the reader to draw on his own associations and imagination to complete the meaning of the poem. In doing so, the dancers will find several layers of meaning in each poem and can thus develop the mood or idea into an extended dance.

Following are a few poems which have been used successfully by high school girls for dance composition.

The first firefly...
But he got away, and I...
Air in my fingers

        (Issa)

Squads of frogs jumped in
When they heard the plunk-plash
Of a single frog

        (Wakyu)

That winter when my
Faithless lover left me
How cold the snow seemed.

        (Jakushi)

We rowed into fog
And out through fog...oh how blue
How bright the wide sea!

        (Shiki)

Butterflies!
Beware of the sharp needles of pines
In this gusty wind!

        (Shusen)

---

[1]*Japanese Haiku.* Mt. Vernon, N.Y. Peter Pauper Press, 1956.

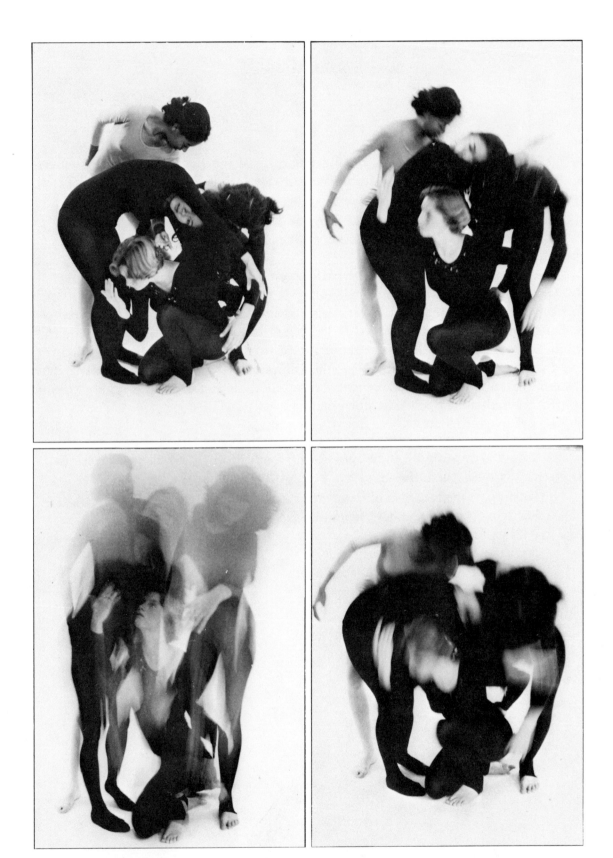

Fig. 30-33. One group's interpretation of the "butterfly" haiku, using a breath lift and drop.

Since my house burned down,
I now own a better view
Of the rising moon.

(Masahide)

The range of mood, quality, and meaning of the foregoing haiku is extensive, from the comedy of cats and frogs to the desolation of winter loneliness. The incorporation of a poem into a dance also has countless variations.

1. *The poem may be read* at the beginning and/or end of the dance.
2. *Each line,* or phrase, of the poem may be read preceding the appropriate part of the dance.
3. *Dancers may speak* words or lines of the poem at the beginning of the dance.
4. *Dancers may speak* words or lines of the poem while they dance.
5. *Key words* may be repeated several times to emphasize the meaning of the dance.
6. *Expressive words* may be added to the poem to provide additional accompaniment. For example, in the haiku about the burning house, the dancers added the word *fire,* repeated several times, to add drama to the first line of the poem. The second and third lines were spoken in slow, melodious tones to provide extreme contrast, which appeared in the movement as well.

In addition to the words of the poem, accompaniment may be used. Haiku poetry seems to stimulate the imagination: in addition to the usual selections of appropriate music, the following have been effectively used:

For frogs: taped sounds of frogs croaking.
For fog: "Psychologically Ultimate Seashore," from the record series
   "The Environments."
For cats: Mancini's "Pink Panther."
For winter: flute improvisations.

Chapter Thirteen
Primitive

Historians tell us primitive people danced for many reasons. Dance was not for exercise or for fun or for entertainment: it was an integral part of tribal life. Dance was communication, history, invocation of nature, and ceremony. Men danced to record great happenings in the life of a tribe: a fire, a tidal wave, a battle, the death of a chief. They danced for the events in a man's life: birth, puberty (the time when boys became men), marriage, death. The mysteries of nature (rain, thunder and lightning, the sun and moon, planting and harvesting) could not be explained in words, so dance was used to imitate, to call forth, or to ward off the mysteries.

Men danced before a hunt, sometimes imitating the hunted animals in movement, in order to insure success. When they returned, they described in movement the marvels of their own bravery and success. (A remnant of this custom can perhaps be found in fishermen's gestures telling the size of the fish that got away.) A tribe going to battle against another tribe would prepare for war with a dance to create unity and belligerence in the group and be rewarded upon return in a dance of victory. Long before cave drawings or verbal legends recorded tribal history, dances were handed down from generation to generation as records of tribal life.

Dance historians such as John Martin, Richard Kraus, Agnes de Mille, Havelock Ellis, and Curt Sachs have written in detail about dance in primitive societies; anthropologists such as Margaret Mead and Ruth Benedict have demonstrated the importance of dance in prehistoric cultures. Perusal of some of these books would be helpful to both instructor and students in preparing to work on primitive dances as a choreographic study. (See the bibliography for the names of some outstanding books on dance history.)

A brief discussion of the role of dance in primitive cultures will stimulate the imaginations of the students in arriving at a theme or idea for a "primitive" dance. Exploration in percussive movement will increase the movement vocabulary needed for these dances. A variety of percussion instruments and records of drum rhythms will provide a choice of accompaniment.

While primitive dances are based on natural events and to some extent imitate natural movements, it must be stressed (as it was in Chapter Ten on gestures) that dance is not merely setting natural movements to rhythm. It is an art form—which means abstraction and change.

You may begin with a natural movement, but you alter it. You change the size, change the part of the body you would ordinarily use, set the movement into a pattern.

If students are going to do a war dance, they shouldn't just pretend to hit each other over the head with clubs—but they may use the same quality of mood and gesture stylized. Primitives did not try to become eagles when they did the eagle dance or lions in a lion dance; they tried to project the quality of the animal in human form. So the students at one further level removed, being sophisticates imitating primitives imitating lions, should realize they can only use the same motivation and starting point—the dance must very much be their own.

THEMES FOR PRIMITIVE DANCE

1. *Daily life:* birth, death, marriage, puberty and fertility rites, selection of tribal chief, planting, harvesting, hunting, and war.
2. *Nature:* rain, thunder and lightning, fire, natural disasters (such as earth quakes, volcanic eruptions, tidal waves), sun, stars, and moon.
3. *Ceremonies* and *celebrations.*
4. *Historical events* in the life of the tribe.

MOVEMENT BASICS

1. *Kinds of movement:* stamps, heel beats, jumps, leaps, strides, turns and whirls; body contractions and pelvic rolls; vibrations and body bounces.
2. *Body position:* crouched low to earth; thrusts into the air.
3. *Louis Horst,* in *Modern Dance Forms,* differentiates between earth primitive and air primitive. The former uses theme, movement, and body positions which are low and close to the earth, while the latter projects the body into the air to represent appropriate themes (fire, sun, lightning, birds).

ACCOMPANIMENT

In terms of rhythmic patterns, primitive percussion accompaniment is usually more involved and more repetitious than jazz. There is usually no melodic line—or if there is, it is somewhat monotonous and is in itself a rhythmic repetitive device. The monotony of sound and movement may build up into an almost hypnotic whole; it is not surprising to find that many primitive dances were intended to, and did, induce trance. (You may wish to refer to chapters Three and Nine for more on percussive movement and appropriate accompaniments.)

1. *Use of drums,* rattles, gourds, wood blocks, sticks.
2. *Use of chants* (authentic or composed by students).
3. *Use of stamps,* claps, slaps, vocal sounds such as cries, shouts, grunts.
4. *Use of records* such as:

    Sandy Nelson—"Beat That Drum" (Imperial 12231) or "Let There Be Drums" (Imperial 9159).

    Daniel Barranjos—"Strictly Percussion" (Record Center HLP 40844 40845).

    Montego—"Authentic Afro Rhythms" (Record Center LP 6060).

    African Music—recorded in Africa by L.C. Boulton (Record Center LCR-57-1367).

    Afro-American Drums (rhythms from Puerto Rico, Bahamas, Haiti) (Record Center LCRA-56-287).

Fig. 34.   Strong percussive movement is typical of primitive dance.

SUGGESTED SEQUENCE
FOR CLASS WORK

1. *Instruction in* and practice of percussive movements, both locomotor and axial.
2. *Improvisation in* and patterning of all types of locomotor movement.
3. *Discussion of primitive dance.*
4. *Division of class* into groups.
5. *Selection* by each group of dance theme.
6. *Selection of type of accompaniment.* If percussion instruments are used, determine whether the dancers themselves will beat out rhythms or other students will provide accompaniment.
7. *Composition of dance,* involving all previously learned elements of choreography.
8. *Presentation* of dance to rest of class.
9. *Evaluation* in terms of quality of movement, clarity of idea or thematic projection, interest, and appropriateness of choreography.
10. *Preparation for performance* (if desired) on the basis of class evaluation and continued practice.
11. *Formation of a longer dance* or dance suite by sequencing several dances, with transitional accompaniment or movement between each section.

Chapter Fourteen

Jazz

An interest in jazz or modern jazz is a fact of life in most high school dance classes. The easy answer for the teacher who has no feel for or background in—or is afraid this aspect will take up all available time and energy—is to indicate that jazz dance is different from modern dance and has no place in a modern dance class. A more productive response is to teach a unit on jazz as though this tradition were just another inspiration for creative work, applying all the choreographic and creative elements emphasized in other approaches. Since modern dance uses any movement the human body can achieve, the jazz idiom is an appropriate inclusion. The instructor should, however, emphasize that the dances the class develops should be modern dances in a jazz idiom, not replicas of show dance or TV extravaganzas.

Jazz, as incorporated into a high school modern dance class, will *not* be the "Charleston" or a chorus line or the "Big Apple" or a tap dance routine. The difference will be not only in the content of the dances but also in the way they are choreographed.

There are two main influences on jazz dance today: European and American. The European style emphasizes an upright torso while the American style uses more hip and ribcage movement, in addition to syncopation and foot-work. The latter emphasis is more appropriate to use in a modern dance class, since the aim is to encourage the use of the whole body.

Basically, however, American jazz dance is derived from primitive dance, although it is less simple and direct. The movement that would be a simple step and arm swing in primitive dance has, in jazz, become longer and more stylized.

PRELIMINARY WORK

Before the students can reasonably be expected to develop their own jazz dance they will need to be familiar with syncopated rhythms, isolations and how they can be used in jazz dancing, and certain characteristics of jazz music and dance.

1. *Syncopation:* accents in non-jazz music usually occur on beat one of a four-beat measure or on beats one and three. In syncopated music accents fall on usually unaccented beats or on the second half of normally accented beats.
Example:

$$\frac{4}{4} \; 1 \; \underset{>}{2} \; 3 \; 4 \; | \; 1 \; \underset{>}{2} \; 3 \; \underset{>}{4}$$

In the next example, the second half of each beat (the & count) receives an accent.

$$\frac{4}{4} \; 1 \; \underset{>}{\&} \; 2 \; \underset{>}{\&} \; 3 \; \underset{>}{\&} \; 4 \; \underset{>}{\&}$$

These rhythmic patterns can be practiced with accented claps or stamps and in walks, with a heel beat or other percussive accent on the syncopated beats.

A useful pattern for practice in hearing and feeling the simple syncopated beat would be:

$$\underset{>}{1} \; 2 \; 3 \; 4 \; | \; 1 \; \underset{>}{2} \; 3 \; 4 \; |$$

$$\underset{>}{1} \; 2 \; 3 \; 4 \; | \; 1 \; \underset{>}{\&} \; 2 \; \underset{>}{\&} \; 3 \; \underset{>}{\&} \; 4 \; \underset{>}{\&} \; |$$

Beat this pattern on a drum, while the class follows the pattern with first claps and then walks. Measure two could involve a body accent on beats two and four while measure four could use heel beats, after each step, on the accented & counts. Other syncopated rhythmic patterns can be constructed and practiced in the same way.

$$1 \; \underset{>}{\&} \; 2 \; \& \; 3 \; \& \; \underset{>}{4} \; \& \; | \; 1 \; \& \; \underset{>}{2} \; \& \; 3 \; \underset{>}{\&} \; 4 \; \& \quad \text{and so on}$$

using both quarter ($\downarrow$) and eighth ($\eighthnote$) notes.

2. *Isolations:* isolations are movements of specific parts of the body, without involving adjacent parts. Isolations are used in both primitive and jazz movement and, indeed, the two kinds of dance are often closely related.

a. Isolations of the head: down, back, sideward, turning, and circular can be practiced in sitting, kneeling, or standing positions.
b. Isolation of the shoulder girdle: up, down, forward, back, and circular—can be practiced in sitting, kneeling, or standing positions, with one shoulder and then with both together.
c. Sideward isolation of the ribcage may be more easily achieved first in a position where the hips cannot move (sitting, kneeling or side-lying). Then the ribcage movement may be tried at the standing level. Working in front of full-length mirrors is most helpful. Lacking these, students can work in two's, checking each other to be sure movement is isolated as intended.
d. The pelvic girdle can move sideward, be tilted forward or backward and be rotated through all four directions. The pelvic isolations can be combined with a walk also: step R on beat one, move R hip

sideward on beat two, step L on beat three, move L hip sideward on beat four.

3. *Jazz quality:* in addition to isolation and syncopation, other elements are inherent to the jazz dance idiom (these are found in other types of dance expression also, of course).

    a. One is *opposition*—if the left arm is diagonally forward, the right arm pulls diagonally back away from the left. If the ribcage is moved to the right, the hips pull away to the left.

    b. This oppositional pull produces a feeling of *elongation* to the line of the movement and *tension* (rather than relaxation) in the entire body.

    c. *Asymmetry,* rather than symmetry, in body line and in group design, will help to make jazz dance more interesting and more appropriate to the modern dance class setting.

Fig. 35.   Jazz quality is emphasized through the use of asymmetry and body tension.

For performance, several jazz dances may be combined in sequence forming a jazz suite, with each dance presenting a different aspect or form of the jazz idiom.

This is not a problem that can be presented to most beginners; because of their lack of experience in a variety of movements they will tend to fall back on what they have seen or experienced in commercial jazz. The more experienced students should quickly be able to apply the underlying concepts of jazz to a greater variety of movement.

Music appropriate for jazz composition:

George Gershwin:	"2nd Piano Prelude"
	"American in Paris"
	"Rhapsody in Blue"
Jimmy Smith:	"Jazz Organ"
	"Hobo Flats" (Verve V6-8544)
	"The Unpredictable Jimmy Smith" (Verve V6-8474)
Gabor Szabo:	"Jazz Raga" (Impulse A9128)

"Afro-American Rhythms" (Record Center LP8040)
"Modern Jazz Movement" (Kimbo 4080)
"N.Y. Export—Jazz" (Warner Bros. 1240)
"Slaughter on Tenth Avenue" (several available recordings)

These records feature compositions in classical or traditional jazz idiom. Dixieland jazz, "cool" jazz, and show jazz are also available in all record shops, providing different sounds for accompaniment.

Chapter Fifteen
Other Art Forms: Painting and Sculpture

While dance does not claim to interpret other art forms, as indicated in the chapter on music (see Chapter Nine, p. 64), both painting and sculpture may stimulate dance composition in much the same way as music does. For a final project for a dance class or for an independent project for advanced students, this can be a challenging assignment. To the instructor the challenge lies in securing the cooperation of the art department and in clarifying the procedure to the students.

PRELIMINARY WORK

1. *Discuss project with art department* and share ideas. If possible, borrow some examples of painting and sculpture which may stimulate movement. Photographs or slides may be used rather than original works or full-sized reproductions.
2. *Discuss with class* ways of translating works of art into dance: the stimulus of color, the spirit or meaning of the original, the line and design of the painting or sculpture. If the painting includes human figures, the starting position of the dance may reflect the positions of the figures in the painting. Excellent examples may be found in the paintings of Diego Rivera. The sculpture of Kaethe Kollwitz entitled "Complaint" is representative of realistic sculpture which may be used in this way.
3. *Ask the class to bring in pictures,* slides, or prints of art works which they think could be used. Possible sources: libraries, art departments, magazines, newspapers, art galleries, museums.

PROCEDURE

1. *Examine* all the examples available with the class.
2. *Allow the class to choose* the pictures or sculptures which appeal to them (using

discretion, of course, in guiding class to the appropriate choice: it's very hard to construct a dance based on a still life of a vase of flowers and a teapot—no matter how much the students may like such a picture).

3. *Divide class into groups* on the basis of these choices.

4. *Each group will decide* the way in which to approach the problem: meaning, form, color, line, design, rhythm.

5. *Each group will select* its own accompaniment: type of music, words, silence, non-musical sound effects, and so on.

6. *Compose dance,* emphasizing the usual elements of choreography.

7. *Evaluation:* emphasis should be placed on the successful relationship of the dance to the original work of art and secondly on the other elements of choreography.

8. *If the dances are of performance caliber,* and are included in a program, projections of the picture or sculpture on a wall or screen in back of the dancers can be effective. An art exhibit of these works may be planned in conjunction with the dance concert.

Fig. 36. Body design which could well be adapted from sculpture.

Chapter Sixteen
Special Seasons

Certain well-marked seasons of the year lend themselves well to being the subject of a program and may serve as the stimulus to choreographic efforts: Halloween, with its black cats, witches, pumpkins and general air of mystery might serve as a starting point for short group studies in class. Thanksgiving has been used, particularly at the elementary school level, for pageants of many kinds, often including dance. However, because of its air of celebration, Christmas is a time of year when many performances are scheduled in the schools and community. Also the holiday falls at a convenient time in terms of the amount of instruction and preparation the dance students have had during the fall term.

CHRISTMAS OR WINTER

The music of Christmas, as well as the connotations inherent in the season, provides a fine impetus for creative work. In a modern dance unit taught at this time of year, a short Christmas carol makes an appropriate finale for the creative work of the class. In a semester-or year-long dance class, the use of a Christmas or winter season theme may provide the first full choreographic effort following various preliminary studies.

One way of implementing the Christmas theme is to start with the selection of music. The range of appropriate music is infinite: from "Deck the Halls" to "Silent Night," from "The Nutcracker Suite" to Bach's "Christmas Oratorios." If each group selects its own music, a well-balanced program will usually result.

Another approach is based on ideas or thoughts about the season. A brain-storming session will produce dozens of words relating to the season which can then be used as impetus for dances. Brain-storming means expressing any idea which comes to mind, relating to the original thought (in this case, winter and Christmas). No ideas are rejected, all are included, and one thought triggers additional contributions from others in the class. A five minute brain-storming with one class produced the following list of key words, many of which were subsequently used as the starting point for dances. Each class will produce its own list, but many of the same words will show up on each list.

Angels	Furry clothes	Ribbons
Bells	Gift wrapping	Rudolph
Candles	Gifts	Santa Claus
Candy canes	Grinch	(and Mrs. Claus)
Carolling	Happiness	Scrooge
Champagne	Holly	Shopping
Chanukah	Ice-skating	Skiing
Children	Incense	Sleighs
Chimes	Jesus	Snow men
Christmas cactus	Joy	(and snow ladies)
Christmas cards	Lights	Star
Christmas tree	Little kids	Stockings
Cold	Love	Three Wise Men
Cookies	Mistletoe	Tinsel
Decorating	Nativity Scene	Togetherness
Eating	(with all the animals)	Toys
Elves	Ornaments	Turkey
Family get-togethers	Parties	Vacation
Fireplace	Plum pudding	Wind
First Christmas	Rain	Worship
Friends	Reindeer	Wreaths

Each group will select a word or series of words for the ideas to be expressed in its dance. The quality or mood will be determined by the ideas—playful, religious, happy, and so on—and then appropriate music or other accompaniment can be selected to assist in designing the dance.

The holiday season presents many opportunities for performance which will be discussed in more detail in Part Four. Preparing completed dances for even informal presentation involves more time and practice than class work. Adequate provision should be made in planning class time so that the dances can be completed, practiced, and performed with authority. The addition of accessories or simple costumes, built on basic leotards and tights, the use of stage sets or set pieces, as well as stage lighting, will contribute to the over-all gala effect.

SPRING

Spring is the time of year when most performing arts classes in high school (music, drama, dance) present a program to demonstrate the year's accomplishments. Parents, friends, and other students are interested in seeing the results of a year's work in class. The spring program can take several forms—it can be based on the ideas of spring, in much the same way as the winter or Christmas program was developed. On the other hand, the dances can be selected from the year's work,

Fig. 37. A fine example of group design.

showing examples of many different approaches to choreography, arranged much as a musical program of varied selections is planned. This type of program will doubtless cover a wide range of dances: serious, comedy, primitive, jazz, blues, as well as some based on concerns and activities related to the school or the community.

Two major objectives are achieved in planning and presenting a culminating year-end program. The school and community have an opportunity to see the work of the dance classes and thus to learn more about the whole field of modern dance. As they come back each year to see the performances, the audience will gain a greater appreciation and knowledge of what modern dance is. Secondly, the dance students are challenged to perfect their compositions for performance in order to fulfill the obligations of a creative art: expressive communication.

Chapter Seventeen
Miscellaneous

A number of other stimuli to creative work in modern dance will be discussed briefly in this section. Don't look at this list as exhausting all the possibilities for approaching dance composition but rather as stimulating your own further exploration. Many of these suggestions are in the light vein, providing a contrast to some of the more serious dances emphasized in previous sections of the book.

These "frivolous" subjects can be used at various times during the year as needed for counterpoint to the solemn approaches. In a program or concert, these light dances also help to balance the menu.

COMIC STRIP AND
CARTOON CHARACTERS

Delightful humorous or touching dances can be built on the characters in popular cartoons or comic strips. This assignment can be given to intermediate or advanced students for duets or small groups. Some examples may stimulate the imagination of the students:

1. *Political Cartoon*

   a. The overly dramatic congressional candidate, haranguing his audience. Both speaker and audience can be danced with movement derived from stylized gestures.

   b. Many political cartoons are not humorous but instead are filled with pathos. One recent example: an inner-city child saying "the man says we should eat less meat. Momma, what's meat?" Such a cartoon can be translated into dance, without words, to emphasize the *feelings* of poverty and alienation.

   c. Another cartoon with dance potential shows a busy mother, cooking with one hand, holding the baby with another and picking up the telephone at the same time—saying to her husband, "Just a minute—I only have three hands." Without being realistic, the dance could portray the frustrations of a harried housewife. Either comedy or pathos could be the approach of this dance.

2. *Comic Strips.* Comic strips are the melodramatic adventures of characters such as Snoopy and Charlie Brown, Little Orphan Annie, or Dick Tracy. Each character in the story should be clearly delineated with characteristic movements, impressionistic rather than realistic. It is indeed possible to tell a story in dance without the use of pantomime.

STORIES

Stories may derive from many sources: from plays, Bible stories, historical events, biographies, the daily newspaper, or personal experience. The process of translating a story into a dance is similar, regardless of the story's source.

1. *The dances should not attempt* a literal translation of the story line, since the words accomplish this more satisfactorily. The central theme of the play or story should be clearly defined in the dancers' minds—is it heroic, melodramatic, humorous, satirical? Does the story emphasize a struggle between two opposing forces? Is the climax a victory for one and a defeat for the other, a compromise between the two opponents or the emergence of a greater force to encompass both? What is the author saying through his words and how can the dancer convey this message through her movement?
2. *Specific characters may be used* (for example, Joseph and the King of Egypt) or representative characters (for example, the Old Man, the Wife, the Prophet, and so on). In either case, the *essence* of the characters should be determined and be the basis for the role just as the *essence* of the story is distilled to give meaning to the whole dance.

FOODS

Even girls who are on a diet enjoy thinking and talking about food—surely there is no more relevant subject matter than this. Usually the "food" dances are fun for the class to work on and fun for the audience to watch.

1. *As in all dance subject matter,* quality of movement should be inherent in the foods selected. The thought of a peanut butter sandwich would not inspire movement as easily as the thought of popcorn popping—although someone *eating* a peanut butter sandwich might inspire a dancer.
2. *A list of "inspirational" foods* follows, with the intention of encouraging expansion of the list.

Popcorn	(popping)
Bacon	(sizzling)
Coffee	(perking)
Bread	(rising)
Champagne	(bubbling)
Ice Cubes	(freezing, melting)
Jello	(jiggling)
Molasses	(spreading, sticking)
Gingerbread Man	(cutting of, baking)

3. *Creative Process*

a. Discuss with class the kinds of foods and drinks which might be appropriate for a dance. Use the above list, if necessary, to stimulate the discussion.

b. Divide the class into groups. Each group may select its own subject matter or may be assigned a food from the list.

c. Discuss use of accompaniment: electronic or novelty music, such as the "In Sound from Way Out" (Vanguard VSD 79222), vocal or other dancer-produced sounds, and percussion instruments are some of the possibilities.

d. Remind the students that the dances are to be choreographed in good form, following all of the precepts previously learned in other creative problems.

e. Ask each group to present its menu component, while the rest of the class guesses the subject.

f. Include some of the dances in a program which has a variety of dances.

TELEVISION

If a single theme is desired for a section of a dance concert or for a whole program, the ubiquitous medium of television may well serve the purpose. Drama and melodrama, news and sports, cartoons and quiz shows, as well as commercials, can provide sufficient inspiration and variety to fill an evening.

No attempt will be made to discuss each category of TV programing separately. A few generalizations will indicate the directions for creative work.

1. *The class should decide* on the areas of programing to be danced:

Soap opera
Weather forecast
Cartoons
Wrestling match
Commercials

2. *Each group may select* the category to be danced, or groups may be formed to create a specific dance ("those who want to work on commercials in this corner," "the sports broadcast over here," and so on).

3. *Each group will decide* on the point of view for its own dance: satirical, comedy, serious.

4. *Emphasis should be placed* on avoiding realistic pantomime or direct imitation of TV shows.

5. *Each dance should incorporate* all the elements of good choreography previously emphasized. Movement should be expressive, original, appropriate, and communicative. Variety in the use of space, time, and dynamics will assist in producing the kind of movement desired.

6. *A script can be written* to unify the program, with an announcer to read and introduce each segment. An alternative procedure might have the script read off-stage while the "announcer" dances the introductions.

7. *Accompaniment can be as varied* as the program itself: taped musical commercials, spoken words, silence, appropriate recorded music, sound effects.

A suggested program follows: Title: *A Day on the Tube.*

1. "Fair and Warmer": *(weather forecast—a dance about spring)* or alternately, "Stormy Weather"—a dance about rain, wind, thunder *(this could be one of the "primitive" dances).*

2. "Riots Continue In—" *(news broadcast—a dance about strife).*

3. "Our Program Will Continue in Sixty Seconds": *(a series of short commercials— commercials can be interspersed throughout the program. Some can even be repeated several times).*

4. "The Doctors and the Nurses": *(soap opera, interrupted by more commercials, of course).*

5. "For Our Younger Viewers": *(cartoons and puppet shows).*

6. "Hollywood Circles" or "College Quiz": *(game shows, winners and losers).*

7. "Musical Matinee": *(the Philharmonic concert—a dance using symphonic or light classical music as the creative impetus).*

8. "Wide World of Sports": *(include several sports-inspired dances: ping pong match, wrestling, marathon walk—this might be a recurring theme throughout the broadcast— karate demonstration, and the like. Special care should be taken in this section to avoid realistic movement).*

9. "Paid for by the Committee to Re-Elect the Senator": *(political announcement— the typical, arm-waving, fist-pounding speaker, perhaps with an audience of clapping automations).*

10. "Wrap-Up": *(the Eleven O'Clock News—a quick recapitulation of all the previous dances, presenting a phrase or two of each dance, to serve as a curtain call for the dancers).*

PART THREE

The Mechanics: Class Organization

Chapter Eighteen
Lesson Planning

To present a formula for lesson planning in modern dance is an impossibility. In addition, it is undesirable, since a creative activity implies creativity on the part of the teacher as well as the students. No two classes will ever be exactly the same, since the students, their personalities, abilities, and previous training, the time, the length of class, and the circumstances will always be different and will always determine the flow of the class. In no way does this excuse the teacher from the necessity of careful planning, but lesson plans are the foundation on which many structures can be built. The instructor must be sensitive to the climate of the class and take advantage of unexpected avenues for creativity or additional technical work.

The instructor's goal and objectives will remain the same throughout the year's program of modern dance, but the implementation and the specific objectives will necessarily change from day to day.

The following is an outline of one way to organize a class session from warming up the class by specific techniques to presenting techniques related to a particular compositional problem and exploring specific elements of time and space—all of them leading to improvisation and composition. Not every class session will include each of these features—probably because of time limitations. Warming up may even be omitted. If the dancers are almost finished with a composition, they may get right into groups and rehearse dance patterns for presenting to the class. There are also times when they don't do much movement at all in a short class; they may sit and listen to music or they may just sit in groups and discuss their compositions. However, this outline gives one of the more logical and comprehensive progressions of class planning.

1. *Techniques* for warming up and physical development of class. Examples:

    a. Bounces and stretches to increase flexibility, coordination, balance, and strength.
    b. Pliés and relevés to improve strength and accuracy of foot and leg movement.

c. Swings—body, arms, and legs—to increase range and freedom of movement.
d. Abdominal exercises to improve control and carriage.

2. *Techniques* for increased movement vocabulary and as basis for specific creative work. Examples:

a. Isolations and percussive movement as basis for primitive or jazz unit.
b. Locomotor movements and patterns as basis for folk-like dances.
c. Sustained movements and patterns of body, arms, and legs as basis for creative work on sustained movement (or "feelings" or Haiku poetry).

3. *Rhythmic training* for improving response to time elements in music and dance. Examples:

a. Response to varying meters, tempos, rhythmic patterns, in locomotor and axial movement.
b. Use of many time elements (accumulative and diminishing meters, phrasing) as integral part of techniques (explaining their use to the students).
c. Use of several forms of accompaniment for techniques (drum, records, tapes, piano, voice).

4. *Space exploration* for increased awareness of the factors which influence movement. Examples:

a. *Controlled changing of levels.*
b. *Use and understanding of directional changes* (body directions and stage directions).

5. *Creative work* to apply all of the vocabulary of movement, dynamics, space, and time to dance composition from the simplest patterns to fully choreographed dances.

a. Each lesson should provide an opportunity for creativity for the students, even before the class is aware of being creative. The ability to choreograph movement does not suddenly appear after an extensive vocabulary of movements has been acquired. Creativity can grow a bit at a time, like a carefully nurtured plant.
b. Examples of first steps in creative development:

(1) Vary a single locomotor movement in direction, quality, tempo.
(2) Combine variations of a single locomotor movement into a pattern.

(3) Add a final measure or phrase to a given pattern.
(4) Improvise on a single movement and then set into a pattern.

Since the major portion of this book is devoted to the step-by-step, building-block approach to creative work, only these few examples are included to remind the readers of this aspect of lesson planning.

6. *"Dessert"* to end the class on a high note of enjoyment or appreciation. Frequently a class draws to a close while dancers are working in groups—it helps to get them together again, no matter how briefly or for what reason. A feeling of completeness or closure can be achieved in several different ways.

a. A few minutes of vigorous locomotor movements with emphasis on fun rather than on form.
b. Presentation and evaluation of completed creative studies.
c. Brief class discussion of studies in progress with suggestions of ways to continue and complete the study.
d. Brief class discussion of some factor of time, space, dynamics, movement, or choreography emphasized in the lesson.
e. Question and answer period—also brief.
f. Announcement of programs and classes in dance which might interest the students. Attention might also be drawn to newspaper or magazine articles of interest.
g. Reports by students of dance programs viewed or classes attended, or relevant stories in newspapers or magazines.

Chapter Nineteen
Class Organization

To emphasize the difference between a dance class and other activity class, informality may be the key note. There is no valid reason for techniques to be practiced in straight lines: quite the opposite is true. Space is used more efficiently if lines are dissolved, allowing the movements of all the students to be more easily observed. The class can also see the instructor more easily. A cue phrase might be: "spread out on the floor so that you are not *directly* in front of, behind, or beside anyone else."

Although the location of the music usually indicates the front of the room (or downstage), the direction the class faces for technical work can be changed frequently for variety and for efficiency. For example, practice in sideward movements is best carried out when the students are facing the long side of the room.

Many students tend to position themselves in the same spots day after day, particularly those who want to be inconspicuous in the back of the room. The instructor can avoid this by moving through the class while they are practicing and then requesting the whole class to turn around to face her at the opposite side of the room.

At times, sharing a gymnasium with another class may be unavoidable. The situation is, of course, undesirable but often may be necessary. In this case, the instructor should face her own class *and* the other class, so that her dancers will have their backs to the other students. Distractions from watching other students, or being watched by them, will be reduced as much as possible.

In teaching and practicing falls and recoveries, which require more floor space than many other non-locomotor movements, the instructor should make sure that students have adequate space. This may be accomplished by having the class face on a diagonal, toward one corner of the room. If necessary, half of the class can perform while the other half of the class watches. Students can learn a great deal from watching each other perform, especially if they are reminded of what to look for. The class may be asked to choose partners to work on many different kinds of techniques: one watches while the other moves, then makes suggestions for improvement. The same dancers should repeat the movement trying to follow the suggestions made. Then the action is reversed.

While lack of space may make this division of the class necessary, an instructor may wish to use the method even though space is adequate. If a class is practicing strenuous activities, such as jumps, they can only do them for a limited amount of time. While part of the students are active, it is helpful to give the others a chance to rest. The ability to watch movement critically can be developed in this way, as well as the ability (or willingness) to accept constructive criticism. And a nice cooperative group spirit is fostered in the class.

For locomotor movements, a variety of formations should be employed rather than always moving in continuous circles. Not only is interest added in this way but also the students experience elements of form, phrasing, and group design. The leg muscles will get some needed rest and the students will learn from watching each other.

Some suggested formations for practicing locomotor movement follow: the solid line indicates where groups move in given pattern; dotted lines show where groups move to get into position for repetition of given pattern.

One group moving in large circle. (Movement is usually counter clockwise.)

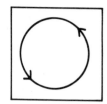

Two or more concentric circles, moving in same direction or opposite direction.

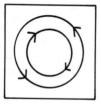

Two or more students at a time move down the center of the room, all movement in the same direction.

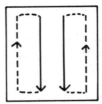

Two or more students at a time move across the room and back again, with the movement they are practicing.

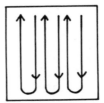

Two or more students move simultaneously from the four sides of the room, either crossing over or moving back to starting place.

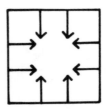

Two groups moving in sequence from two corners of room, movement always from the same two corners.

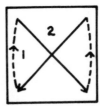

Four groups, moving in sequence diagonally, from four corners of room, keeping to own right as they approach opposite corners.

Chapter Twenty
Groupings for Creative Work

Beginners in a dance class, attempting their first creative problems, should usually work in groups of five to eight. The self-consciousness of performing alone or in small groups is thus eliminated. The ideas and contributions of many students will make creative effort easier and lay the groundwork for procedures to be used throughout the creative aspects of class work.

If given free choice, students will naturally gravitate into groups with those they know best and the groups so formed will repeat themselves for each creative project. The instructor will find that methods of work and movement patterns also repeat themselves when the same girls work together time after time. To get fresh inspiration and to get acquainted with all members of the class, students should be encouraged to form new groups each time. The usual objections are that "we work better with our friends," "I can't express myself with girls I don't know."

The instructor should be prepared to point out the advantages and the necessity for changing groups: to become acquainted with everyone in the class, to get new ideas from new people, to learn to adapt to other students, to appreciate the contributions made by various students. The instructor may find it necessary to use a number of different methods to arrange new groups. A few teacher's objectives and methods are suggested below, some of the methods depending on chance and some on a more contrived random selection.

OBJECTIVES

Students will learn:

1. *To work* with many different members of the class.
2. *To accept groups* which include others than their own "cliques" or friends.

3. *To appreciate* the ideas and contributions of all members of the group.
4. *To become* both a leader and a follower in creative work.
5. *To accept new ideas* and new points of view.
6. *To accept random selection* gracefully.
7. *To appreciate* the need to include the unpopular or unskilled members of the class.

METHODS

1. *Count off by numbers,* according to total number of groups desired. For example, in a class of forty students count off by eights, to divide class into eight groups of five each.
2. *Use of roll sheets* in various ways:

   a. First five on roll will be group one, and so on.
   b. First, third, fifth, seventh, and ninth girls will be group one, and so on.
   c. Random selection of names from roll sheet, for example, numbers 1, 40, 4, 37, 20. This method may be used by instructor to break up cliques, without emphasizing the process. Balance in the composition of groups may also be achieved, balancing creative ability, technical ability, and "followers."

3. *Basing new groups on previous groups:* if there were eight groups of five on the first creative project, there might be five groups of eight on the second. One member of each old group will be assigned to the new groups so that no two girls will be working together a second time in succession.
4. *Random selection* by group number: slips of paper with group numbers, letters, or names are placed in a box (or on the dance drum). Each girl takes a slip of paper and joins others with same numbers at a specific place in the room.
5. *Selection of groups by specific members of class:*

   a. One girl selects three or four others she has not worked with previously. Continue for as many groups as required.
   b. Selection as in "picking teams"—"captains" pick the girls in turn. If this method is used occasionally for variety, secret selection will avoid embarrassment to those picked last. An alternate method: each captain chooses one member for her group. On the second round, each captain takes a name from the alphabetical roll sheet, thus combining choice and random selection. Third round is free choice again, fourth round alphabetically from the roll sheet and so on until all members of class are placed in a group. The "captains" may be selected by various methods also. A few suggestions:

(1) Vote of the class.
(2) Random selection by instructor.
(3) All members of one previous group.
(4) All second-year dance students, in a mixed class of first-
and second-year students (if applicable).
(5) All students with the same first name (if applicable).
(6) All students wearing same color leotard (if practical).

6. *Division into groups according to subject matter* for the creative approach. For example, in the TV dances suggested on pp. 95-96, the dancers interested in commercials could form one group; another group could be set up to work on the soap opera, and so on.

PART FOUR

Dance as a Performing Art

Chapter Twenty-one
Dance Production

Since dance is a performing art, classes in modern dance should culminate in performance. The annual spring recital, dear to the hearts of music and dance teachers in schools and studios, is only one among many possible opportunities for performance. The ability and desire to perform for an audience can be developed in class work, in the same way that the ability to create in movement is developed. Each time one group presents a study or pattern to the rest of the class... *there* is a performance. Thus the very first group efforts in creative work are also preparing the dancers for the separate roles of performers, audience, and critics.

This chapter covers, in ascending order of formality, difficulty, and importance, different types of dance productions and particular ways of making each of these an experience in appearing before an audience.

PRESENTATION IN CLASS

1. *Delineate floor area* in which dance or pattern is to be presented. Downstage is usually where the accompaniment is placed, but it need not always be in the same place in the room.
2. *Seat audience* (rest of the class) in downstage area.
3. *Discuss with class* the specific elements of choreography to watch for (depends, of course, on the particular study being presented).
4. *Emphasize the role of the audience*—to watch, to appreciate, to react, to criticize (preferably constructively). Discussion or review of own dance are inappropriate while another group is performing.
5. *Emphasize the role of the performers:* to *dance* their pattern as if it were the greatest ever created, without verbal or physical apology.
6. *Evaluation:* each group which performs should receive some evaluation from class and instructor. As the students learn more about form, style, design, dynamics, and so on, they will become more knowledgeable as critics.

Statements such as "I like it," "I don't like it," "Linda didn't know what she was doing," should be avoided. Students should be encouraged to explain *why* they liked it and what they did not like. General, rather than specific, comments about the performance are more acceptable (for example: "Some of the girls in the group seemed to be watching the others while they danced").

The instructor will usually summarize the evaluations by the class and then add her own. Just as fragile flowers need encouragement to grow and blossom, so, too, do dancers need encouragement to create and perform. Therefore the instructor should emphasize the good points of each presentation and make suggestions for improvement, encouraging the students to recognize and build on their success and eliminate the less successful elements.

PERFORMANCE FOR OTHER PHYSICAL EDUCATION CLASSES

To enlarge the audience, a second step in performance might be for the dancers to perform for all the Physical Education classes scheduled in the same period as the dance class. Either an informal or formal presentation may be made. For example, on a rainy day when the usual activities are disrupted, the other P.E. classes might be invited to watch what the dance class is doing.

1. *General suggestions for informal presentation:*

   a. Encourage dancers to *dance* to the best of their abilities regardless of size of audience.
   b. Explain to the audience what the dancers used as their starting point for this particular creative problem.
   c. Make sure that the audience understands the role of an audience.
   d. Allow time for questions and/or comments from the audience.
   e. Reserve class evaluations until only the dance class is present.

More formal (or at least, planned) intra-class performances are ones that are scheduled in advance and may take several forms.

If a beginning class is not ready for full-scale performance, a special program of "works in progress" might be planned for other P.E. classes during the same period. The studies or dances would be in a more completed form and be presented as a performance.

The general suggestions listed above are also applicable here.

An elaboration of this type of performance has been used at several schools at Christmas: a program of seasonal dances (see Chapter Sixteen in Part Two) is presented each period during the day for all the other Physical Education classes (both male and female).

2. *General suggestions for formal presentations:*

a. Make sure that all groups which have completed their dances have the opportunity to perform at least once during the day.

b. Allow dance classes to decide which dances should be performed once and which six times (if there are six periods in the school day). A simple ballot form can be used and the results tabulated and announced (see below).

c. Obtain cooperation of administration and faculty to excuse the dancers from other classes on day of performance.

d. Seek cooperation of physical education staffs to educate audience in advance for courteous behavior.

e. Plan for enough time in class to complete and practice dances for performance.

f. Arrange for lighting with drama department if possible.

g. Suggest a few elements of costuming to add to basic leotards and tights if desired.

h. Arrange dances on programs for variety and contrast; be sure that one of the better dances is used to end the program.

GROUP NAME OR NUMBER	NUMBER OF PERFORMANCES						
	0	1	2	3	4	5	6
1.							
2.							
3.							
4.							
5.							
6.							
7.							

PERFORMANCES FOR SCHOOL ORGANIZATIONS

Most high schools have a Parent-Teachers Association or Parents Club providing support for student activities. If a dance teacher is invited to present a program or part of a program for a meeting of one of these organizations, she should try to accept. She has a rare opportunity to expose a group of interested parents and teachers to modern dance and at the same time to repay the organization for its concern and support (in the past or in the future). In addition, the more the dancers perform, the better the performances will be. General suggestions:

1. *Select dances from class projects* which will be enjoyable for a lay audience and yet will present a clear picture of what modern dance is and what it hopes to accomplish.
2. *Explain each dance,* either in terms of a starting point for its creation or in the meaning of the dance. These program notes may be spoken (by instructor or student) or may be in a printed program.
3. *A brief explanation* of what modern dance is and how it is taught may be appropriate as part of the spoken material.
4. *A few dances* might be included in a general program which is devoted to physical education or one which is devoted to all the performing arts.
5. *Program chairmen* often welcome volunteered programs and a dance instructor may wish to suggest a program of the kind mentioned here.
6. *Back-to-school-night or an open house* (in various forms at different schools) offer an opportunity for dancers to perform and for parents to see the results of class work.

PERFORMANCE FOR ASSEMBLIES

Different schools have various traditions in regard to assemblies: some schools schedule assemblies on a regular basis, others have assemblies or convocations to present special speakers or programs from outside the school. Between these two extremes are innumerable variations. New traditions can be established, one of which might be a Dance assembly.

At one school, this may be a Christmas program presented for the whole school or the Spring concert presented during an assembly period. At another school, a "Girls' Assembly" is presented each year, with music, dance, fashions, and recognition of athletic and scholastic achievement incorporated into a program for girls only.

The values of school assembly programs are:
provides opportunity for dancers to perform; exposes the school to modern

dance as a performing art; arouses interest of many more students in joining the modern dance classes.

General suggestions:

1. *Select dances* which are well-choreographed and well-rehearsed.
2. *Select dances* which will have a wide appeal: "fun" dances, dances using contemporary accompaniment, dances which have meaning to a general high school audience.
3 *Introduce and explain the dances,* in simple terms, either in a printed program or spoken (student or faculty announcer or Master of Ceremonies).

PROGRAMS WITH OTHER DEPARTMENTS IN THE SCHOOL

Interdepartmental cooperation is essential in any school situation and particularly so in the performing arts. A dance teacher may cooperate with the drama and music departments by choreographing the school's musical comedy production. The drama teacher may reciprocate by lighting the dance productions and assisting with sets or stage pieces. The music department may provide accompaniment (orchestra, jazz band, choral groups) for some major dance compositions. Dance, drama, and music are so closely related that a department of the performing arts is a distinct possibility in some schools.

For performance, a program of music, dance, and drama may supplement or replace a full-scale dance concert.

General suggestions:

1. *Plan far in advance* with other departments involved, for a well-balanced program.
2. *Select a location* (auditorium, multi-purpose room, outdoor theater, or gymnasium) which will provide the best possible staging for all the performers.
3. *Coordinate the program* so that some of the selections involve more than one department, for example:

a. Dancers compose a dance to jazz band accompaniment or to vocal accompaniment;
b. Music group provides accompaniment or background music for musical comedy scenes or a one-act play.

Further interdepartmental cooperation may result in a Fine Arts Week or a Festival of the Performing Arts. A week-long schedule might include performances by the drama, music, and dance departments, with a home economics fashion show and an art department show added for increased variety, participation, and interest. One such program is outlined below:

Festival of the Performing Arts

Monday	Fashion show, with musical interludes by small groups, solo, duets
Tuesday	Concert: orchestra, choirs, and madrigal groups
Wednesday	Dance concert
Thursday	Gymnastics and judo demonstrations
Friday	Variety (or talent) show
Saturday	Drama presentation
Sunday	Jazz concert: jazz band, stage band, soloists

PROGRAMS WITH OTHER SCHOOLS

In a school district that has several high schools or in an area where several independent high schools are relatively close together, a joint dance concert has many advantages. A full evening's program of dance can be presented without the stress and strain falling on a single teacher and her classes. Each group has the opportunity to view and appreciate other approaches to dance composition. Cooperation without competition is enhanced, the audience is expanded, with parents and friends of the dancers from several schools in attendance.

General suggestions:

1. *Advance planning* is essential. If practical, a meeting of the dance teachers from the participating schools should be held several months in advance. In some areas, regular meetings of the high school dance teachers are scheduled throughout the year, to share ideas and to plan master classes, informal workshops, and formal programs.
2. *The host school* (which can be rotated each year) is responsible for arrangements such as tickets, lights, printed programs, dressing facilities, rehearsals.
   Each school should publicize the concert as fully as possible.
3. *Each school* should know how many dances they are to present or how much time is allotted for their portion of the program.
4. *An over-all theme* may be established well in advance. Some possibilities:
   "We Dance America"
   "Dance Through the Ages"
   A dance history of _____ (city, town, or geographical area)

5. *Arrange numbers on program* for greatest interest, variety, and contrast.

6. *Discuss their role* as an appreciative audience with all participants.

7. *The educational aspects* of a cooperative program, as opposed to a competitive attitude, should be emphasized with all dancers in advance.

8. *If at all possible, a dress rehearsal* should be scheduled to insure a smooth-running performance.

9. *A follow-up meeting for evaluation* of the whole program is highly advisable.

Chapter Twenty-two
Demonstration Group

Many teachers have found value in assembling a demonstration group, using a whole class, dance club, or selected members of several classes. Such a group would be rehearsed and available for performances of many kinds at any time during the year.

In an area or school district where only one high school has a well-developed dance program, the demonstration group might be invited to other high schools to stimulate and assist in the development of a dance program at those schools. School and community organizations can be encouraged to invite the demonstration group to appear on various programs. The purpose, of course, goes beyond mere entertainment into the realm of improving the audience's knowledge and appreciation of the art of dance.

It is interesting to note that Martha Graham's 1974 Spring season in New York took the form of a lecture-demonstration, rather than her more usual dance concert. According to Don McDonagh,[1] Hanya Holm first introduced the lecture-demonstration form in the early days of modern dance to explain to an uninformed public the vocabulary and methods of Mary Wigman's technique. This method remains a highly educational and effective procedure. Miss Graham used the lecture-demo for many years, elevating it to a "minor art form."

In a recent season, she introduced her company in a "typical" Graham class, describing and explaining the technique and movements performed by her dancers. Excerpts from many of her famous compositions followed, with one complete dance masterpiece to end the program. For Miss Graham, who at age 80 no longer dances, her presentation was a form of retrospect. For the high school teacher who is still trying to educate an audience, the lecture-demo has the same validity it had for Graham, Holm, Humphrey, and Weidman in the 1920's and 1930's.

[1]McDonagh, Don. *Martha Graham*. N.Y. Praeger Publishers, 1973. p. 87.

FULL-LENGTH DEMONSTRATION

In a full-length demonstration, the program might include:
1. A technique demonstration.
2. Improvisations—individual and group.
3. Short studies, with various choreographic approaches.
4. Completed dances.

For shorter programs, parts 2 and 3 could be eliminated, with a technique demonstration preceding the presentation of dances. A lecture-demonstration is an excellent educational device, allowing more time for background explanation of both technique and composition than a program devoted to performance exclusively.

1. *Technique demonstration.* The purpose is to "show lay groups some of the many kinds of movement which students use to become creative dancers!"

General suggestions:

a. Determine, from length of entire program, how long the technique demonstration or technique series should be.
b. Follow the technique demonstration described in Appendix C or select appropriate movements to include. Each instructor may wish to develop her own demonstration to highlight the techniques used in class.
c. Use of several groups moving in sequence allows for a variety of movement without exhausting the participants.
d. Use of several groups in sequence also allows for a heterogenous class: Group I may perform a simple form of each technique while groups II, III, and IV demonstrate more advanced forms.
e. Music may be taped, with phrases selected from many sources, to provide correct meters and tempos or the movements may be adjusted to allow the use of a single record for accompaniment. An accompanist who can improvise at the piano provides the most desirable accompaniment but most high schools are not so lucky as to have one.
f. A technique *series* differs from a technique *demonstration* in being shorter in length (perhaps three or four minutes), continuous in movement, performed in unison, and naturally less inclusive. For a short demonstration program, the technique series serves as a "warm-up" for the dancers and an introduction to movement for the audience.

2. *Improvisations.* Improvisations can be very risky but they can also be very exciting to both performers and audience. Some students improvise readily and

---

[1]Jones, Ruth and DeHaan, Margaret. *Modern Dance in Education*, N.Y., Teachers College Press, 1948, p. 11.

well; others lack the freedom to do so, especially in front of an audience. Many classroom experiences in improvisation will help the students to be freer in improvising. However, each instructor can determine the advisability of including improvisation in her demonstration program. One argument in favor of including it when possible is that it helps to show the audience the origins of many creative ideas.

General suggestions:

a. In technique demonstration (Appendix C), several ways of improvising are included—any or all may be adapted to any demonstration group.
b. Select specific areas of movement, space, time, or dynamics for improvisation.
c. In preparing the group for demonstration, improvisation in class, in advance, may be helpful. But to keep the true freedom of improvisation, patterns should not be planned in advance.
d. During a demonstration program, be ready to guide the improvisation if necessary or even to terminate it if the class seems to be floundering. But try it again later or at a future demonstration.
e. Group improvisation can be highly effective.
f. Group composition can also be effective: give the group an assignment (for example, a food, a color, an emotion, a space limitation) allow ten minutes for work and then present to the audience. While the dancers are creating, the instructor can talk with audience or answer questions.

3. *Short studies.* The purpose of this section of a demonstration is to indicate some of the many possible approaches to creative work. The selection should cover as wide a variety as time permits. The narrator can explain briefly the starting point for each brief study and perhaps indicate how each could be expanded into a longer composition.

General suggestions:

a. Select areas of choreography which are not included in the improvisations.
b. If a specific movement is the starting point for the study, select a movement which was used in the technique demonstration and indicate how it developed creatively.
c. Select studies which demonstrate many creative approaches. For example: one movement, one space element, one time element, one poem, one gesture, and so on.
d. Despite the brevity of these presentations, each should demon-

strate the principles of good choreography: use of groups, variations in time, space, and dynamics, clarity of idea, and so on.

4. *Completed dances.* All of the previous parts of the demonstration culminate in the final section of the program: completed dances. Although dances choreographed by the instructor might be more exciting or more professional, such dances would not present a clear picture of the goals of modern dance in a school situation. Technique, improvisation, and short compositional studies all lead to group creation of dances in class work. Since the lecture-demonstration reflects class procedure, the final section of the program should be dances composed by student groups.

General suggestions:

a. Select a few dances (time will determine the number) which are original, exciting, and interesting to the audience (the best the class or club has to offer).
b. If possible, use groups of various sizes: a duet or trio, a group of five, a group of eight or nine.
c. Introduce each dance by title with a few words of explanation if necessary.
d. Costumes or accessories added to the basic leotard and tights used for the rest of the demonstration can be very effective—but costume changes should not produce long delays between numbers.
e. End the lecture-demonstration with a planned "bow" or curtain call for all the participants. Doris Humphrey emphasizes the importance of the bow:

> "The bow is the end after the ending and is extremely important as the final statement of the dancer. I believe bows should be composed carefully, even if they are to look spontaneous and natural. Of all the elements in a bow, space awareness is the most important....Bows should differ according to the dance they follow....Students must be trained in these procedures and encouraged to think about and work on the proper bow, not leaving this important affair to a last-minute dress rehearsal."[1]

---

[1]Humphrey, Doris *The Art of Making Dances.* New York: Holt, Rinehart and Winston, 1959. pp. 88-89.

Chapter Twenty-three
Other Aspects of Production

In the early days of modern dance, costumes, properties, lights, stage sets, and makeup were eliminated from the consideration of the dancer—part of the revolt against both ballet and the Denishawn School of expressive, ornamental dance. Today dancers and choreographers consider all the aspects of a production in relation to the whole effect of the dance on an audience. A high school performance can become a production through the judicious addition of appropriate lighting, costuming, and staging.

Since many high schools do not have an auditorium, a cafetorium, multi-purpose room, or gymnasium must frequently be used for dance concerts. The gymnasium is often more desirable since the floor is easier on bare feet than many stages or the tile floors in the cafeteria. Another advantage is the bleacher seating—uncomfortable, surely, but providing a much better view of the dancers than the flat-floor seating of a multi-purpose room. An auditorium (with a large, smooth hardwood stage, comfortable seats with good sight lines, adequate stage lights, and backstage space) is not usually available to the high school dance group. Therefore the gymnasium must be converted into a concert hall through the use of ingenuity and the cooperation of other departments.

LIGHTING

General suggestions:

1. *Cooperation* of the drama department or drama club, which utilizes lighting for its productions, is essential.
2. *Portable footlights* can be set up to define the stage space in a gymnasium or multi-purpose room.

3. *Fixed spotlights* (frenelles) can be hung from basketball backboards in gym or from ceiling in multi-purpose room.

4. *A moving spot* is helpful and effective in highlighting individual or small group movement.

5. *Colored gels* which can be changed assist in emphasizing the quality of the dances.

6. *The lights* can be operated by members of the drama class or club or by members of the dance class or club, to provide worthwhile experience in the technical aspects of theater production.

7. *A list of the dances* on the programs should be provided for each light operator — with suggestions as to light colors and intensity, or a brief description of the meaning and desired effect of the dance.

8. *The student choreographers* of each dance frequently have ideas of how the lights can contribute to the over-all effect of the dance (for example, start in darkness, bring lights up slowly, change from blue to red at the climax, and the like). Dancers should be encouraged to think about lighting as a contributing factor to their dance.

9. *The colors of the lights* (gels) should be selected to emphasize the colors of the costumes rather than to negate them.

10. *Strobe lights* and black light can be highly effective for specific kinds of dances — but should be used sparingly to achieve maximum eloquence.

11. *If a printed program is provided* for the audience, the "house lights" should be brought up between dances so that the audience has the opportunity to read the program.

COSTUMING

Since most dance classes use a basic leotard and tights as appropriate dress for class work, costumes for performance can be built on this basic outfit. Dances are often presented in unadorned practice clothes. However the addition of accessories or costume pieces will greatly enhance most dances. The students should be encouraged to use ingenuity instead of large expenditures to devise costumes for their dances.

General suggestions:

1. *As the dances are choreographed,* discuss with class elements of costume which can be added to the leotards and tights to emphasize the meaning of the dances.

2. *Accessories* should never be added to a leotard just for the sake of adding something: a scarf or sash or flowing sleeves (for example) should be related to the dance itself and not be extraneous to its meaning.

3. *Each group* can be responsible for providing its own costuming or a committee can be selected to design and execute the costumes for all the dancers.

4. *The home economics department* is frequently helpful in both designing and constructing costumes.

5. *Money-raising projects* (candy or bake sales, a car-wash, and the like) may be necessary to raise the money if costumes are expensive. On the other hand, departmental funds, gate receipts, or parents' organizations may provide needed funds.

6. *All costuming details* should be considered in terms of the movement of a dance: a head covering which slips or falls during dance movement should be secured or eliminated; a long skirt may look beautiful on a posed figure but trip a moving dancer.

7. *Costuming* should be considered as an enhancing element for the dance as a whole rather than as a separate decorative feature.

8. *Students* should be encouraged to minimize a costume, to *suggest* a full costume rather than to *use* a full costume. For example: one full sleeve and one full pant-leg are more effective to delineate a clown costume than the full clown outfit would be.

9. *Asymmetry in costuming* (a stripe of color on one arm or one leg instead of both) is usually more effective.

Specific suggestions:

10. *Scarves:* one of the most useful of costume accessories: can be used as a head covering, as a collar, as a sash, as a skirt or a drape.

11. *Bands of color:* use of "magic" tape which will adhere to leotards and tights is a simple and effective device. Other materials can be basted to the leotard to achieve a similar result: strips of sequins, ropes of tinsel or yarn, and so on.

Some designs might be:

a. Single stripe, starting from wrist, up the inside of the arm, down the length of body and leg to the ankle.
b. Single stripe on outside of one arm and outside of other leg.
c. Bands of color around neck, wrist, or ankle.
d. Zig-zag lines of color on leotard.
e. Spiral bands around arm, leg, or body.

12. *Skirts may be worn* over leotard and tights, or over leotard without tights. Skirts can be of any length appropriate to the dance. A long skirt provides lovely flowing lines for lyric movement, but care should be taken that it will not interfere with changing levels or locomotor movement. A skirt which hides movement rather than enhancing it should be avoided. Skirts for dance can be elasticized at the waist or tied on so that the problem of fitting them to each dancer is minimized.

Effective skirts can also be made by attaching strips of various kinds to a belt or waistband. The strips can be of crepe paper, of scarves of different colors (or all one color), of dyed sheets or unbleached muslin, of ribbons of various widths. Such skirts are usually worn over leotards and tights, in matching or contrasting

colors; without in any way inhibiting movement, a skirt-like effect is obtained.
13. *Dance dress:* a one-piece dance dress is another solution to costuming. The dress may be designed to be worn over a leotard or over dyed-to-match-briefs. The skirt may be of any length suitable to the dance, the top may be fitted, bloused, or loose. The sleeves may be short, long, or non-existent. The most important factor, as always, is how well the dancer can move in the dress; the material and design must move with the dancer. Jerseys or stretch materials are most appropriate for these purposes. Since these costumes are apt to involve a larger investment than simpler accessories or costume pieces, the dresses should be designed to be used over and over, year after year.

A variation of a dance dress is the pinafore, made to wear over a basic leotard. For a folk-like dance or a "Raggedy Ann" dance, the pinafore might be short with ruffles over the arms, made of an inexpensive print. For a Pilgrim or frontier dance, the pinafore might be midi or full length, with simple lines and neutral colors. Unbleached muslin is a useful material for skirts and pinafores since it is relatively inexpensive, dyes easily, and has enough body to drape well.

14. *Boleros and vests:* a small part of costume may represent or intimate the full costume. This is especially true of boleros or vests worn over leotard and tights. A bolero may be used to suggest a Spanish, gypsy or Calypso costume. The design is simple and can be executed in a variety of materials. A bolero does not restrict movement yet adds to the impression desired.

A vest usually is closed in the front rather than open like the bolero. A vest may button or hook up the front (snaps are not advisable although tight-closing grippers can be used) or be zipped up the back. A jazz dance might use a striped vest, a choreographed minstrel show might use vests of different colors.

The lines of the vest can be varied also: V-neck, round neck, turtleneck; it could be ribcage length, waist length, or hip length, depending on the type of dance being costumed.

15. *Other costume pieces:*

> a. Collars: a scarf or bandana tied around the neck is the simplest type of collar available — yet it is definitive for certain kinds of dances: folk-like dance, cowboy dance, hoe-down.
>
> > Other collars can be designed and cut and sewed to accentuate other kinds of dances —
> > Turtleneck (jazz)
> > Ruff (medieval)
> > Cowl neckline (religious or preclassic)
> > Formal pointed collar (ballroom type or jazz)
>
> Worn over leotard and tights, with or without other costume pieces or accessories, collars can be just the hint needed to clarify a character or a dance to the audience.
>
> b. Sleeves and legs: just as a collar can represent a whole costume, so can sleeve or pant-legs. The sleeve may be of diaphanous chiffon

which emphasizes lyrical arm movement. It may be made of ribbons, attached to a band at wrist and shoulder (tacked to shoulder seam of leotard, if necessary). "Leg-of-mutton" sleeves (full at the biceps and tight below the elbow) could represent a Victorian era costume.

In many dances, a single sleeve rather than two sleeves is desirable. As indicated previously, asymmetrical design is more exciting than symmetrical; this applies to costuming as well as choreography. The dancers and the instructor would do well to consider which type of design is more appropriate for specific dances. Pants or single pant-legs follow the same design principles as sleeves. They can serve as costume accents worn over leotard and tights or as a full costume with leotard or other blouse or shirt tops. Some examples:

> (1) For a sailor dance, authentic navy blues or whites can be used, with perhaps a red tie or kerchief to break the regulation uniform picture.
> (2) For a cowboy or western dance, jeans or cut-off jeans could be used, with color accents such as a bandana around the neck or in the back pocket.
> (3) For a clown or puppet dance, a single, full, unbleached muslin pant-leg could be used; appropriate appliques or painted designs could be added.
> (4) For a "dreamy" dance, a pair of full pants of light material such as chiffon, could be worn instead of a skirt.
> (5) For a "harem" type dance, a pair of full pants with elastic at the ankle (or a single pant-leg, made the same way), again of a flowing material, might produce the desired effect.

16. *Paint:* An inexpensive but striking costume can be achieved by using water soluble paints on leotards and tights. Lines or designs can be painted directly onto the basic outfit; water soluble and quick drying paints are available in all colors. Small figures or patterns will not show up under stage lights so the use of paint should be in bold designs, in bold contrast to the color of the leotards. An occasional use of fluorescent paint and black lights can be most effective. Suggestions made for bands of color (p. 127) could be followed in using paints.

17. *Accessories:* Accessories include all kinds of costume accents which can be added to basic leotard and tights or to other constructed costumes. Included would be items such as jewelry, gloves, and headgear.

a. Jewelry should only be worn if it is part of the costume. Dancers should be requested to remove all of their everyday jewelry (rings, bracelets, necklaces of all kinds) since they catch the light and are distracting. Certain kinds of selected jewelry are appropriate as part of a costume if they do not distract from the movement. For example, bracelets or anklets of shells, beads, seed pods, or bells might be used for a Primitive or Afro-Haitian dance. A large, but lightweight, brooch or pendant might accent a dance based on Pre-Classic forms, Medieval concepts, Biblical stories, or Greek mythology. As in all costuming, the jewelry should be selected to enhance the dance rather than to be the focal point of interest.

b. Gloves of many kinds may be used as costumes accents for many kinds of dances, with the usual discretion since they focus attention on the hands. Some examples: colorful mittens, scarf, and hat added to leotard and tights would make a complete costume for one of the dances about winter fun. Short white gloves, with a large gaudy ring worn over one glove, accented a dance based on the gesture of "come here." Opera-length gloves might be used for one of the Pre-Classic court dances such as a Sarabande or a Minuet.[1]

c. Headgear includes not only hats and scarves worn on the head but also decorations worn in the hair. The most important consideration, aside from appropriateness, is that the headgear stay on the head or in the hair and does not fly off onto the stage or into the audience (very distracting!). Many high school girls are very clever in arranging different kinds of hair-do's and the total costume effect can be greatly enhanced by how the hair is arranged and decorated. (A word of caution: for class work, it is a good idea to insist that all students use rubber bands, barrettes, clips, or whatever is needed to keep their hair out of their faces. One of the easiest habits to learn and one of the hardest to break, is the dancer's habit of pushing her hair out of her face when she doesn't know what else to do. This carries over into performance and can be devastating to unity of effect of a dance.)

Some examples of appropriate hair decorations: garlands or wreaths of flowers or leaves for spring or a love dance; ribbon or yarn on pigtails or ponytails for a children's dance or a western dance; Christmas tree decorations (tinsel, icicles, and the like) for a "fun" Christmas dance; a comb or mantilla for a Spanish or gypsy dance; a headband for an American Indian or other tribal dance.

Most of these costume suggestions require more imagination and ingenuity than financial outlay, which is as it should be. The students will always come up with new and worthwhile ideas if they are given a few appropriate hints.

18. *Stage sets*

The term stage sets is used loosely here to include any structure or form added to a bare stage or gym floor. These include devices to delineate the stage area as well as forms used as a part of a dance. On a stage, backdrops, front curtain,

---

[1]See Horst, Louis. *Pre-Classic Dance Forms.* New York, Kamen Dance Publishers. 1953.

and side curtains are usually available. In a gymnasium or multi-purpose room, none of these are present. Ingenuity (and cooperation from drama or industrial arts departments) can fill the gap.

a. Movable folding screens, if available, can be used to permit side exits and entrances for dancers as well as to mark upstage limits and form a background for movement. Stage flats can be set up to serve the same purposes, although this requires more effort. Portable acoustical shells used by music departments are sometimes available to provide a background.

b. The dancers themselves can also be used to provide a background; this device has been successfully used when large numbers of dancers are performing All groups pose in the background whenever they are not performing. The poses, emphasizing various levels and body positions, are held motionless through each dance. The poses of each group can be changed as one dance group exits and the next group takes the stage.

c. If projections of any kind are used in the program, a large screen, center upstage, will serve the double purpose of marking the stage area and showing projections. The projections can be specific for each dance or abstract color, line, or design for background. Smaller hanging screens can be used to receive projections from the back, as with overhead **projectors**.

d. Specially constructed pieces can contribute to the overall effectiveness of a dance if they are incorporated into the choreography of the dance. Martha Graham collaborated for many years with eminent stage designers such as Arch Lauterer and Isamu Noguchi, pioneering in this area of choreography as she did in so many other areas. The elaborate structures used professionally would be impossible and inappropriate for high school production but simple levels, boxes, cubes, and free-form pieces can be easily built and effectively used. Sawhorses, balance beams, vault boxes, volleyball poles, cage balls, stacks of gymnastic mats, and other equipment already available have been used imaginatively to provide settings for various dances.

One school has used a free standing skeletal picture frame to introduce each dance. At Christmas, this was used to present "Christmas Cards" to the audience. Each group assumed a pose inside the picture frame as the dance was announced and then stepped forward through the frame into its starting position. This simple device can be used in a variety of forms and serves to unite the disperse elements into a whole production.

Hand props should not be overlooked as contributing elements in dance composition. Any object held or carried by dancers is included in this category. They may be realistic objects (broom, whip, wooden spear, nylon parachute) which help to delineate a character or the meaning of a dance. A cord, rope, or chain might contribute greatly to a dance about enslavement and freedom. Specially constructed abstract forms, carried or held or passed around by the dancers, are also effective devices. In fact, such forms may be the creative stimulus for a dance instead of a contributing factor.

However, instructor and students should not be carried away by the excitement of working with hand props or stage props. These are primarily devices to enhance composition, not to replace good movement and good choreography.

19. Makeup

a. Stage makeup
A final additional touch to dance production is the use of makeup. As is true of all elements of production which have been discussed, makeup is not necessary for the success of a dance. It can, however, add a finishing touch. Since stage lights tend to wash out natural skin tones, a liquid or pancake facial makeup is needed to achieve a healthy natural look. Eye makeup (shadow, liner, and mascara) will help to make the eyes appear more expressive. Even though many high school girls do not usually use lipstick, it does help to counteract the blanching by stage lights.

b. Body Paint
For special effects, special makeup may be used. War-paint for Indian, primitive, or tribal dances is very effective, if not overdone. For dolls or puppets, red cheeks, freckles, drawn-on eyelashes may be considered as part of the costume. For clowns or various mimes, some variations of their traditional makeup may be used.

If male dancers are dancing bare-chested, body makeup may be necessary. An overall color may be used to counteract the light-induced paleness, or body paint in colors may be used for special effects.

c. Glitter
Sequins or other kinds of glitter are sometimes used instead of eye shadow, when appropriate for the dance. These decorations can be affixed to the face with white glue or vaseline for easy removal.

Variety in makeup is fun to use—as always, the dancers will have some new and exciting ideas. Good taste and appropriateness should be the deciding criteria for limiting the use of makeup; it must add to, not detract from, the dance itself.

Fig. 38. A stunning example of group choreography from the dance "Revelations" by the Alvin Ailey Dance Company.

CONCLUSION

The creative aspects of dance have now been dissected, analyzed, but hopefully not dried out. Each element of dance composition has been suggested, discussed, and outlined. It would appear that an over-all recipe for dance composition could now be used, for example, a cup of Part One, a tablespoon of Chapter Four, a pinch of Section Two, beat well together and bake for half an hour in a hot oven. Luckily there is no recipe and this book is not the *Joy of Cooking.*

It might be titled the *Joy of Dancing,* however, because without joy on the part of the instructor and the students there is no dance. Performers, maybe, but no dance. It would be better to violate every choreographic principle and have the dancers *dance* their joy in moving than to have a perfectly constructed composition which the dancers "walk through."

Martha Graham has said that movement must have "passion" to become dancing—a fine legacy for a young dancer.

Appendices

Appendix A

Glossary

The terms in the glossary are defined in relation to their use in the text.

Accumulative Meter: (also called cumulative meter) regular increase in number of beats in succeeding measures.

Affective Domain: the area of learning concerned with attitudes, interests, feelings, values, appreciation, and imagination.

Amplitude: (see RANGE)

Asymmetry: an element of design based on uneven balance of parts.

Axial Movement: movement in space, over a fixed base (body movement).

Choreography: the art of creating dances.

Cognitive Domain: the area of learning concerned with acquisition of knowledge and ideas and the mental abilities and skills to use the knowledge in problem solution.

Contour: the shape or outline of body or group in space.

Contraction: a pulling together in the center of the body, so that ribcage and hips are brought closer to each other.

Counterpoint: the simultaneous combination of two or more "voices" (melodies or movements).

Cumulative Meter: (see ACCUMULATIVE METER)

Diminishing Meter: (also called decumulative meter) regular decrease in number of beats in succeeding measures.

Direction: the path of movement in space and the relation of the body to stage space.

Distortion: an exaggeration of or change from the natural.

Focus: that point toward which attention and movement are directed.

Gallop: a forward or backward locomotor movement with same foot leading each step. Gallop consists of step and close, performed in an uneven rhythm ($\quarternote$ $\eighthnote$) with the feet brought together and weight transferred in the air.

Hop: a locomotor movement performed on one foot; take off from and land on same foot.

Jump: a locomotor movement performed on both feet; take off from and land on both feet. Jumps may emphasize elevation or distance.

Kneeling Position: weight is supported on either one or both knees (see photo on p. 13).

Leap: a locomotor movement with a transfer of weight from one foot to the other, with the transfer of weight occurring in the air. A leap differs from a run in that the time in the air is extended as long as possible. A leap may emphasize distance (length) or height (elevation).

Level: height in reference to floor, ground, or stage; in dance, reference is usually to position of body: lying, sitting, kneeling, or standing.

Locomotor Movement: movement through space, over a moving base. Movement in which the body goes somewhere.

Lying Position: body weight is supported on back (supine position), front (prone position), or on either side of body.

Meter: the primary rhythm or fundamental beat per measure of music or dance.

Opposition: an element of design referring to straight lines and angles.

Percussive Movement: sharp, beating movement. Force is applied in an explosive impetus with little or no follow-through.

Phrase: a unit of melody (music) or movement (dance)—usually 4 or 8 measures.

Prance: a variation of a run, in which the knees are lifted high.

Primary Rhythm: (see METER)

Psychomotor Domain: that aspect of learning concerned with body movement and activity and the control of physical movements to solve a problem or reach a goal.

Range (Amplitude):   the relative size of movement in space, from large to small. A given movement may be performed with varying degrees of amplitude.

Resultant Meter: the pattern of accents which results from simultaneous use of two different meters, creating a third, combination meter (see pp. 20 and 61).

Rhythm: the organization or structure of music or movement in time.

Rhythmic Pattern: the melody of music or the foot pattern in movement, based on the meter and using combinations of long and short beats. Sometimes called secondary rhythm.

Run: a transfer of weight from one foot to the other, with a moment during which both feet are off the floor simultaneously as the weight is transferred.

Secondary Rhythm: (see RHYTHMIC PATTERN)

Sitting Position: weight is supported on one or both hips. For various sitting positions, see photo on p. 12.

Skip: a step-hop combination, alternating feet on each step. Rhythm is uneven: ♩♪.

Slide: a sideward locomotor movement in an uneven rhythm. Consists of a step and close (♩♪) with the transfer of weight taking place in the air as the feet are brought together; same side leads in a series of slides.

Standing Position: weight is supported in one or both feet. Since the base is small, great variety is achieved through different positions of arms, body, and feet with flexion or extension of knees and hips.

Succession: an element of design referring to curved lines.

Suspended Movement: body movement, usually sustained, with an added feeling of lift or breath which holds body in air.

Sustained Movement: continuous, smooth movement; force is applied with no differentiation between impetus and follow-through.

Swinging Movement: swaying or rocking movement, responding to the pull of gravity, usually following curved lines. The impetus is a tipping off balance with the follow-through in an arc or long curve.

Symmetry: an element of design based on equal balance of parts (both halves of a design are identical).

Syncopation: displacement of accent, which falls on a usually weak or silent beat or part of a beat.

Tempo: the rate of speed.

Vibratory Movement: a series of short, quick percussive movements, performed in rapid succession, producing a trembling or shaking effect.

Walk: a transfer of weight from one foot to the other with one or both feet in contact with the floor at all times. Used synonymously with *step*. Walks may be performed in any direction, with infinite variations.

Appendix B
Learning Objectives and Evaluation

It's easy to create learning objectives for techniques and learning objectives for knowledge, but constructing learning objectives for the creative aspect of dance is difficult—that is to say, objectives the attainment of which can be measured.

Measuring progress in any creative field is a subjective process. Each teacher and each student will have her own opinion about what has been learned and what should have been achieved. This is determined by the background in dance and related art fields.

However, for those who would like to set some specific objectives—regardless of the way in which their achievement may be measured—the following summary may provide a few guidelines.

To summarize the contributions of dance to the educational process as a whole:

I. Contributions to the growth of the individual student

    A. Physical (psychomotor)

        1. Development of coordination, strength, flexibility, poise, rhythm, control.
        2. Use of the **whole** body.
        3. Physiological benefits derived from a comprehensive physical activity.
        4. Increased aliveness in the body, producing a sense of physical well-being.

    B. Mental (cognitive)

        1. Understanding of dance as an art form.

2. Understanding of music as related to dance and as a separate art form.
3. Knowledge of costuming in relation to dance and to art principles in general.
4. Increased knowledge of all the arts through study and use of principles common to all art forms.
5. Knowledge of movement terminology, space and time principles, fundamentals of choreography, history of and personalities in modern dance.

C. Social (affective)

1. Creative experience affording an emotional and expressive outlet.
2. Appreciation of varied contributions to group by many individuals.
3. Experience in roles of leader and follower.
4. Accepting responsibility for a group project and one's own contribution to it.
5. Improved acceptance of evaluation and the ability to evaluate constructively and objectively, both one's own actions and those of the group.
6. Increased feeling of security through group membership and performance.
7. Appreciation of other art forms through experience in the art of movement.

II. Contributions to the aims of general education

A. Integration of intellectual, emotional and physical aspects.
B. Development of imagination and personal creativity.
C. Integration of learning the arts, the social sciences, theater, language arts. Development of awareness of outside world and the continuity and flow of civilization, with an understanding of modern times as a product of the past.
D. Develop enjoyment of life-time activity with tremendous carry-over value in all three domains: cognitive, psychomotor, and affective!

The most extensive exposition of performance objectives to date has been prepared by Project C.O.P.E. (Cluster VII Movement and Dance Concepts) Department of Education, Tallahassee, Florida. This booklet may be ordered from Panhandle Area Educational Cooperative, 412 South Boulevard, Chipley, Florida 32428 ($3.10 includes postage).

---

[1]Adapted from Jones, Ruth & Margaret DeHaan. *Modern Dance in Education*. N.Y., Bureau of Publications, Teachers College, Columbia University, 1948 (used with permission of publisher).

EVALUATION

Evaluation is an integral and important part of education. Various methods of evaluation, to determine fulfillment of objectives, may be employed. Written tests (true-false, multiple choice, matching, completion, and short essay questions) will help to determine cognitive learning: definitions of basic dance vocabulary, space and time elements, dance history, design, and choreography.

A few sample questions follow:

True or False

(T) 1. *Locomotor movements go from one place to another.*
(F) 2. *Unevenly balanced design is called symmetry.*
(T) 3. *Amplitude refers to the size of movement.*
(F) 4. *Tempo means time or rhythm.*
(T) 5. *Sustained movement is slow and continuous with even application of force.*

Multiple Choice (circled *all* of correct letters)

1. A skip is

   (a.) a combination of step and a hop

   (b.) a locomotor movement

   c. in an even rhythm

   (d.) in an uneven rhythm

2. Pioneers in the development of modern dance include:

   (a.) Martha Graham

   (b.) Doris Humphrey

   (c.) Charles Weidman

   (d.) Hanya Holm

3. Space elements used to make movement more interesting include:

   (a.) Focus

   (b.) Level

c. Meter

(d.) Direction

4. The following principles of art *do not* apply to dance choreography:

a. Balance

b. Variety

(none)

c. Contrast

d. Unity

Short Essay

1. What are some elements of choreography you look for in evaluating a dance?
2. What are some of the values of *performing* your dances in class or for an audience?
3. Discuss elements of time which are commonly used to vary movement in composition.
4. What is improvisation and why do we use it in class?

In constructing tests, the teacher should keep in mind that some students may be beautiful dancers and highly creative without being able to read, understand, or answer comprehension questions.

Evaluation in the psychomotor domain can be accomplished through skill testing, with several students performing at once.

A few examples of skill testing follow:

1. Student shall be able to perform any of the basic locomotor movements, as requested by the instructor, in appropriate form and rhythm. Example: Given a drum beat or appropriate music, the student will be able to perform a *skip* with body extended, feet pushing off from the floor, arms either held in position (sideward at shoulder height) or swinging with control in opposition to legs.
2. Student shall demonstrate ability to perform basic axial movements, as requested by instructor, in appropriate form and rhythm, at different levels. Example: Given

a drum beat or appropriate music, the student will be able to perform a series of two-beat swings, emphasizing the curved line and rebound of true swinging movement. The swings may be performed at a single level (for example, standing) or at several levels in succession (for example, standing, kneeling, sitting).

3. Student shall perform a combination of at least three locomotor movements, either a pattern assigned by instructor or one devised by students. Example: Instructor assigns locomotor pattern of four skips forward, four slides to the right, two step-hops forward, four jumps in place. Students are graded on accuracy, grace, and quality of the movement pattern. Example: Student shall perform a locomotor pattern four measures in length, including at least three different locomotor movements with at least two changes of direction. The patterns may be devised and performed individually or in groups of two or three students.

4. Dances (or shorter patterns) shall be evaluated by class and instructor on basis of an evaluation sheet, provided by instructor. Class discussion may be substituted for written evaluation when deemed appropriate.

Much evaluation of dances or studies will occur in discussion following class work. Occasionally, a more structured evaluation may be desired. The following evaluation sheet can be used for detailed analysis of short studies or longer dances. One sheet is given to each member of the class, with space provided for her to evaluate ten groups. A plus or minus may be used to answer each question or a qualitative grade may be indicated, using letter grades (A-F) or numbers (1-5) as desired by instructor.

Any section may be eliminated if inappropriate or other concepts may be substituted or added.

Evaluation in the affective domain remains subjective despite efforts to objectify. How does one determine changes in attitude objectively? How does a teacher record the contributions from various group members to a completed dance project? Is it possible to determine quantitatively the experience of students as leaders and followers in a dance group? Can responsibility, appreciation, enjoyment be measured on a scale? We all know that students in a creative dance class change and develop in the area of attitudes, feelings, and social experience. The judgment of the teacher remains as the best source for such evaluation.

Students may be asked to discuss in class some of the learnings they have achieved in the affective domain. Such a group discussion is appropriate following a performance or on a "short-period" day when class time is cut to a minimum. The instructor may also wish to include a short essay question on a final exam relating to this area of learning. For example: We all know that modern dance provides good physical exercise. What are some of the other things you have learned in this modern dance class?

Students should be encouraged to think about the question and answer as fully as possible. This type of question could also be included in a take-home final, in which case a longer answer would be expected.

Fig. 39-42. As part of the evaluation process, students should be encouraged to look at movement from the point of view of the audience. Some movements are seen better from the side, some better from the front. The movement shown in Figs 39-40 is seen better from the side (Fig. 40); the movement in Figs. 41-42 is seen better from the front (Fig. 42).

EVALUATION OF DANCES		Number of Group									
		1	2	3	4	5	6	7	8	9	10
Fulfill problem?												
Movement	Varied?										
	Unusual?										
	Interesting?										
	Appropriate?										
Rhythm	Accurate?										
	Varied?										
	Phrasing?										
Levels	Changing?										
	Contrasting?										
Directions	Changing?										
	Appropriate for movement?										
Contour of Group											
Focus	Appropriate?										
	Conscious?										
Continuity	Does movement flow?										
Performance	Is it *danced* with authority?										

Comments:

Name_____

Date_____ Period_____

Appendix C
Technique Demonstration

AXIAL MOVEMENT

I. BODY BOUNCES

Forward, R, backward, L. Accumulative meter: 4 meas. of

$\frac{8}{4}$; 4 meas. of $\frac{4}{4}$; 4 meas. of $\frac{2}{4}$; 8 meas. of $\frac{1}{4}$.

3 groups: standing, kneeling, sitting. All 3 groups move simultaneously.

Group I. Standing

Starting position: stride stand, body erect, arms at sides.

A. *Bounce* body forward toward floor by bending forward from hips, trunk and knees remaining straight, arms extended sideward at shoulder height. 7 small bounces.   7 cts

   Recover: stretch to erect starting position, arms remaining extended sideward at shoulder height.   1 ct   8 cts

B. *Bounce* body sideward to R by tilting body to R side (movement is directly to side without flexion at hips) with L arm stretched overhead beside L ear and R arm stretched across body to L at about waist height. 7 small bounces.   7 cts

   Recover: swing L arm down in front of body, then swing both arms sideward at shoulder height while body returns to erect position.   1 ct   8 cts

C. *Bounce* body backward by bending at knees, keeping body in straight line from head to knees, hands placed just below buttocks, helping to push hips forward and prevent flexion at hip joint. 7 small bounces.   7 cts

   Recover: return to erect position by extending knees, arms extended sideward at shoulder height.   1 ct   8 cts

D. *Repeat* movement B above to L side, reversing direction of body tilt and arm positions.   8 cts

Repeat movements A, B, C, D, with 4 cts for each part.   16 cts
Repeat movements A, B, C, D, with 2 cts for each part.   8 cts
Repeat movements A, B, C, D twice through, with 1 ct for each
part.   8 cts
Note: On 1 ct bounce, recovery occurs on *and* after ct 1.

Group II.   Kneeling

Starting position: kneel stand, body erect over knees, arms at sides.
Movements A, B, C, D, as described for Group I, are performed by
kneeling group in same rhythm.   64 cts
Forward bounces are taken by flexing at hip joint so that but-
tocks almost touch heels. Back remains straight.
Sideward bounces are taken as described for standing group.
Range of movement is limited by narrow kneeling base.
Backward bounces are taken by leaning body backward in a
straight line from knees. Arms are brought forward to shoulder
height in front of body to maintain balance.

Group III.   Sitting

Starting position: hurdle sit with L leg flexed in front of body (outside of leg on floor) and R leg flexed backward (inside of leg on
floor), body erect, arms at sides.

Movements A, B, C, D, as described for Group I, are performed by
sitting group in same rhythm and in same manner. Range of   64 cts
movement in all directions is limited by starting position.

2. SIDE SWING AND FALL

1 meas. of $\frac{15}{8}$ meter. (Each count given below is equal to three eighth
notes.)

3 groups: standing, kneeling, sitting. All 3 groups move simultaneously.

This follows the bounce series, and the starting position is the
one in which the bounces end: body erect, arms extended sideward at shoulder height.

Group I.   Standing

Starting position: feet in stride position, body erect, arms extended
sideward at shoulder height.

A. *Swing* body and arms to R, weight on R leg, arms beside ears.
Body remains facing forward, not turning to side.   1 ct
B. *Swing* body and arms downward and then up to L side, weight
over L leg, arms beside ears.   1 ct
C. *Swing* body and arms downward and then up to R side, lifting
L leg from floor, with flexed knee.   1 ct
D. *Fall* to L side by quickly lowering body and arms to R, flexing
hips and knees, then, as L lower leg and foot touch floor, swing-

ing L arm across in front of body to L and sliding L arm and body out on floor. Position at completion of fall is an extended side-lying position on L side. Knees do not touch floor in falling.

2 cts   5 cts

Group II.   Kneeling

Starting position: kneel stand, body erect over knees, arms extended sideward at shoulder height.

A. *Swing* body and arms to R side, weight over R knee, arms beside ears. Body remains facing forward.

1 ct

B. *Fall* to L side by flexing hips, swinging L arm downward and across in front of body to L and sliding L arm sideward to L along the floor with body following to extended side-lying position on floor.

1 ct

C. *Recover* to kneel stand position by pulling body up from side-lying position, leading with sideward and upward movement in rib-cage and continuing upward to kneel.

1 ct

D. *Repeat* swing to R.

1 ct

E. *Repeat* fall sideward to L.

1 ct   5 cts

Group III.   Sitting

Starting position: hurdle sit, body erect, arms extended sideward at shoulder height.

A. *Swing* body and arms to R side, weight over R hip, arms beside ears. Body remains facing forward.

1 ct

B. *Fall* to side by swinging L arm downward and across in front of body to L, sliding L arm along floor to L, body following to extended side-lying position.

1 ct

C. *Recover* to sitting position (same technique as for kneeling group).

1 ct

D. *Repeat* swing to R.

1 ct

E. *Repeat* fall sideward to L.

1 ct   5 cts

Transition: All move simultaneously. *Roll* (¼ turn to R) onto back, lying with legs extended, arms extended on floor sideward at shoulder height.

2 cts

3. SWINGS FROM LYING POSITION

8 meas. of ⅜ meter. There are 2 movement counts in each meas. of ⅜ meter, falling on the 1st and 4th beats.

All move simultaneously.

Starting position: back-lying, legs extended, arms extended on floor sideward at shoulder height.

A. *Swing* up into long sit position. Impetus for movement is in chest, with arms swinging forward to assist movement, ending with arms extended in front of body at about shoulder height.

1 ct

Recover: swing down again to back-lying position, by contracting abdominal muscles, rounding back, then unrolling back to extended position on floor, while arms move back to floor and slide out to extended position sideward at shoulder height.

1 ct   2 cts

B. *Repeat* swing up and down.   2 cts
C. *Swing* up to sit, facing R diagonal: body twisted to R side,
weight largely on R hip, arms parallel and reaching to R of
body.   1 ct
  Recover: swing down to back-lying position by same action
described above.   1 ct   2 cts
D. *Swing* up to sit, facing L diagonal: reverse C position.   1 ct
  Recover: swing down to back-lying position.   1 ct   2 cts
Repeat movements A, B, C, D.   8 cts
Note: Recovery to lying position after last swing up (to L diagonal)
  is omitted, and a change of position, to the starting positions
  described below, is substituted. All groups face forward.

4. BODY BOUNCES AND STRETCHES
32 meas. of $\frac{4}{4}$ meter.

4 groups: in sitting positions described below. Each group does
  own pattern alone first; then all 4 groups repeat their own patterns simultaneously.

Group I.   Frog Sit
Starting position: sitting with soles of feet together, knees flexed,
  back erect, hands on ankles.
A. *Bounce* body forward, back rounded, head moving toward feet.
4 small bounces.   4 cts
  Recover: straighten back, keeping body as low as possible, re-
turning to erect position with straight back.   4 cts   8 cts
B. *Bounce* body forward, keeping back straight, movement occur-
ring at hip joint. 4 small bounces.   4 cts
  Recover: round back (by contracting abdominal muscles and
flexing spine), and then unroll back to erect position. (Movement
is made by extending spine successively from base of spine to
head; head is last part to be straightened.)   4 cts   8 cts

Group II.   Long Sit
Starting position: sitting with legs extended together in front of
  body, back erect, arms at sides.

Movements A and B as described for Group I.   16 cts

Group III.   Stride Sit
Starting position: sitting with legs extended in wide stride, diagonally forward from body, body erect, arms at sides.
A. *Bounce* body forward with rounded back, over R knee, head
moving toward knee, arms stretching overhead and forward,
body turned to R. 3 small bounces.   3 cts
  Recover: straighten body quickly to erect starting position, arms
stretched overhead.   1 ct   4 cts

B. *Bounce* body forward between legs in manner described in movement A. 3 small bounces. — 3 cts

    Recover: as described for movement A. — 1 ct — 4 cts

C. *Repeat* movement A over L leg, with recovery. — 4 cts

D. *Repeat* movement B, bouncing forward, with recovery. — 4 cts

Group IV.   Stride Sit with Partner

Starting position: stride sit (as described for Group III), facing partner; partners join hands and sit so that partners' feet are touching, with legs in as wide stride as possible.

Circle with partner: one starts backward to R side, other starts forward to L side; continue with large body circle, describing circle as close to floor as stretch in legs allows. 1 circle. — 8 cts

    Repeat. — 8 cts

    Transition: All move simultaneously. Slow change to ½ *long sit* position, facing L wall. — 2 cts

5. SUSTAINED HIP THRUST AND EXTENSION WITH ROLLS

6 meas. of $\frac{4}{4}$ meter—slow tempo.

All move simultaneously.

Starting position: ½ long sit, L leg extended forward on floor, R foot on floor near buttocks with R knee flexed, back erect, L hand on floor behind L hip, R arm flexed and held between flexed knee and body.

A. *Extend* body upward by thrusting hips upward from floor, R arm reaching toward ceiling. Movement is sustained and finishes with body in full extension, facing toward ceiling, weight held on L hand, L foot, and R foot. — 2 cts

    Recover: return to starting position by lowering hips to sit position and flexing body at hips. Movement is sustained. — 2 cts — 4 cts

B. *Repeat* extension and recovery. — 4 cts

C. *Roll* to L by extending to back-lying position with both legs extended on floor, arms stretched overhead or flexed in front of chest; then take 2 slow rolls, ending in same ½ long sit position described above. — 4 cts

D. *Repeat* movements A and B. — 8 cts

E. *Repeat* rolls, rolling to R, ending in side-lying position on R side, facing forward. — 4 cts

6. LEG SWINGS IN LYING POSITION

16 meas. $\frac{6}{8}$ meter. (See comment on $\frac{6}{8}$ meter, p. 151.)

All move simultaneously.

Starting position: lying on R side, legs and body extended, R arm stretched overhead, L hand on floor in front of chest to aid in maintaining balance. Contracting abdominal and gluteal muscles will help to achieve strong extension in entire body as well as in supporting leg and to establish balance in side-lying position.

A. *Swing* L leg forward from hip, knee straight, foot extended. 1 ct
Swing L leg backward from hip, knee straight, foot extended. (Leg remains parallel to floor and equidistant from it throughout swing.) 1 ct
5 more *swings* (making a total of 7), alternately forward and backward. 5 cts
Recover: roll quickly to L into reverse position on L side, raising L arm overhead as roll is taken. 1 ct   8 cts

B. *Repeat* forward and backward leg swings with R leg, and repeat roll to R, ending with both arms extended overhead. 8 cts

C. *Swing* both legs and both arms forward (legs and arms straight) into jackknife position. 1 ct
Swing both legs and both arms backward (legs and arms straight) into completely arched position.. 1 ct
4 more *swings* (making a total of 6), alternately forward and backward. 4 cts
Recover: roll quickly to L into reverse position on L side. 2 cts   8 cts

D. *Repeat* forward and backward swings. 6 cts
Recover: omit roll, coming up to long sit position, facing forward. 2 cts   8 cts

7. HIP-WALKING
24 meas. of $\frac{4}{4}$ meter.

3 groups: all in long sit position; each group moves forward in turn, then all move backward simultaneously.

Group I
Slow rhythm: equal to ½ note for each "step."
Starting position: long sit, legs extended together in front of body, body erect, arms extended in front of body at shoulder height.
Walk forward on hips by lifting hips alternately from floor, starting with R. Slow rhythm permits high lift and hold before replacing one hip and lifting other. 8 "steps." 16 cts

Group II
Moderate rhythm: equal to ¼ note for each "step."
Starting position: long sit, legs extended together in front of body, body erect, arms extended in front of body at shoulder height.
Walk forward on hips by lifting hips alternately from floor. 16 "steps." 16 cts

Group III

Fast rhythm: equal to ⅛ note for each "step."

Starting position: long sit, legs extended together in front of body, body erect, arms extended in front of body at shoulder height.

Walk forward on hips by lifting hips alternately from floor. Movement should be very quick and sharp. 32 "steps."   16 cts

Groups I, II, and III

Walk backward on hips by lifting hips alternately from floor.

    8 "steps," slow rhythm.   16 cts
  16 "steps," moderate rhythm.   16 cts
  32 "steps," fast rhythm.   16 cts

Transition: Backward *somersault* landing on hands and feet, facing R wall. Somersault may be modified so that instead of turning over, body pivots on buttocks with knees to chest, then changes to crouch position on all fours. It is suggested that entire group use same method of transition to ensure uniformity of appearance.   2 cts

8. WALKING ON ALL FOURS

6 meas. of ¾ meter.

2 groups: each group moving alone first, then both groups moving simultaneously, with Group I doing Group II's previous movement and Group II doing Group I's previous movement.

The movements may be named "Inchworm" and "Hoptoad."

Group I

Starting position: weight on hands and feet, body crouched.

A. *Walk* hands forward, alternating R and L; feet remain in place, so that body ends in complete extension, weight still on hands and feet. 4 "steps."   4 cts

B. *Walk* feet forward, alternating R and L; hands remain in place, so that body ends in crouched starting position. 4 "steps."   4 cts

Group II

Starting position: weight on hands and feet, body crouched.

A. *Lift* both hands (weight held on feet) and place them down farther forward.   1 ct

B. *Lift* both feet (weight held on hands) and jump them forward to starting position.   1 ct

Alternate movements A and B 3 more times (making a total of 4).   6 cts   8 cts

Groups I and II

Repeat, each group performing other group's previous movements. Rise to standing position, facing forward, on ct 8 instead of completing movement.   8 cts

9. HIP THRUSTS

2 meas. of $\frac{4}{4}$ meter each for Group I, III, and IV. 2 meas. of $\frac{5}{4}$ meter for Group II.

4 groups: standing, each group moving in turn.

Group I

Starting position: standing with feet together, body erect, arms at sides.

A. *Step* diagonally forward to R with R foot.   1 ct
B. *Step* forward with L foot, bringing feet together.   1 ct
C. *Bend* knees, thrusting hips forward simultaneously. Heels come up from floor, arms brought up in front of body below shoulder height to help maintain balance.   1 ct
D. *Return* to starting position by extending knees and straightening body, bringing arms to sides.   1 ct   4 cts
Repeat movements A, B, C, D, starting with L foot, facing diagonally forward L.   4 cts

Group II

Starting position: standing with feet together, body erect, arms at sides.

Movements A, B, C as described for Group I.   3 cts
D. *Hold* position with flexed knees and hips thrust forward.   1 ct
E. *Return* to starting position in manner described for Group I.   1 ct   5 cts
Repeat movements A, B, C, D, E, starting with L foot, facing diagonally forward L.   5 cts

Group III

Starting position: standing with feet in wide stride, body erect, arms extended sideward at shoulder height.

Note: Tempo is very slow. Movement is slow, sustained, and controlled, contrasting with sharp percussive movement of other groups.

A. *Bend* body forward from hips, back remaining straight.   1 ct
B. *Flex* knees as deeply as possible.   1 ct
C. *Thrust* hips forward slowly over knees as body slowly returns to erect position; knees gradually extend also.   2 cts   4 cts
Repeat movements A, B, C.   4 cts

Group IV

Starting position: standing with feet together, body erect, arms at sides.

A. *Leap* forward on R diagonal, leaping onto R foot.   1 ct

B. *Jump* in place, bringing L foot up to R. Simultaneously bend knees and thrust hips forward over knees. Heels come up from floor; arms are brought up in front of body below shoulder level to help maintain balance.   1 ct

C. *Return* to starting position by extending knees and straightening body, bringing arms to sides.   1 ct

D. *Hold* starting position.   1 ct   4 cts

Repeat movements A, B, C, D, starting with L foot, facing diagonally forward L.   4 cts

10. SUSTAINED AND PERCUSSIVE MOVEMENT

8 meas. of slow $\frac{3}{4}$ meter for Group 1; 12 meas. of slow $\frac{3}{4}$ meter for Group II; 1 meas. of slow $\frac{4}{4}$ meter and 2 meas. of slow $\frac{3}{4}$ meter and a repeat for Group III; 6 meas. of slow $\frac{4}{4}$ meter for Group IV.

4 groups: standing, each group moving in turn.

Group I

Starting position: standing with feet in wide stride, body extended, arms extended diagonally forward and upward from shoulders, palms facing downward.

A. *Push* downward with hands, entire body following movement. Knees flex as hands and body are lowered toward floor. There should be a feeling of pushing downward against great resistance.   3 cts

B. *Push* upward with hands (palms up), entire body following movement. Knees extend as body returns to starting position.   3 cts

C. *Circle* body to R, arms remaining beside ears. To describe complete circle, knees flex and body comes close to floor between legs, then knees extend again as body completes circle toward L side.   6 cts   12 cts

Repeat movements A, B, C.   12 cts

Group II

Starting position: standing with feet in wide stride, body extended, R arm extended diagonally forward and upward from shoulder, palm facing downward, L arm at side.

A. *Push* down with R arm, entire body following movement. (This is same movement as A for Group I, using 1 arm rather than 2.)   3 cts

B. *Push* upward with L arm (palm up), R arm remaining at side. (This is same movement as B for Group I, using 1 arm rather than 2.)   3 cts

C. *Repeat* downward push with L arm.   3 cts

D. *Repeat* upward push with R arm.   3 cts

E. *Circle* body to R, as described in C for Group I. Circle starts with R arm overhead; L arm is brought overhead as circle progresses. At end of body circle, R arm is stretched upward and L arm is at side, as in starting position, for repeat.   6 cts   18 cts

Repeat movements A, B, C, D, E.   18 cts

Group III

Starting position: standing with feet together, body extended, R arm
   extended diagonally forward and upward from shoulder, palm
   facing downward, L arm at side.

A. *Push* downward with R arm, entire body following movement;
   step forward simultaneously with R foot. This is a percussive
   thrust downward.   1 ct
B. *Push* upward with L arm, entire body following movement;
   step forward simultaneously with L foot. This is a percussive
   thrust upward.   1 ct
C. *Repeat* downward thrust with L arm, stepping forward with R
   foot.   1 ct
D. *Repeat* upward thrust with R arm, stepping diagonally forward
   and sideward with L foot, into side stride position.   1 ct
E. *Circle* body to R, as described in E for Group II.   6 cts   10 cts
Repeat movements A, B, C, D, E.   10 cts

Group IV

Starting position: standing with feet together, body extended, arms
   extended diagonally forward and upward from shoulders, palms
   facing downward.

A. *Push* downward with hands, entire body following movement;
   step forward simultaneously on L foot. This is a percussive
   thrust downward.   1 ct
B. *Push* upward with hands (palms up), entire body following
   movement. This is same sustained push upward described for
   Group I, movement B.   3 cts
C. *Circle* body to R, arms overhead, stepping diagonally forward
   and sideward with R foot into stride position. Body circle is
   initiated with sideward push or impulse in rib-cage, so that
   arms move very slightly to L before beginning circle to R.   8 cts   12 cts
Repeat movements A, B, C.   12 cts

II. SWINGS IN STANDING POSITION

8 meas. of ⅜ meter. (See comment on ⅜ meter, p. 151.)

All move simultaneously: 8 figure-8 swings, each swing increasing
   in dimension.
Starting position: standing with feet in stride position, body erect,
   arms at side.
1st *swing* is forward contraction of shoulders, arms following movement forward, back of hand and outside of forearm facing forward. As shoulders move back on 2nd half of swing, arms are rotated outward, back of hand and outside of arm also leading
   swing backward. Arms thus describe a figure-8 forward and
   backward.   2 cts
Succeeding 7 *swings* increase in dimension by adding flexion and

extension of knees and whole body to swing of shoulders and arms. Knees and body flex as arms move forward, arms crossing in front of body to make first loop of figure-8. Knees flex and body extends as arms move down, back, and upward in circle for 2nd loop of swing. 7 swings.

| | 14 cts | 16 cts |

12. SIDE SWINGS

20 meas. of $\frac{6}{8}$ meter. (See comment on $\frac{6}{8}$ meter, p. 151.)

2 groups: 1 standing, 1 kneeling. Both groups move simultaneously, performing same movements on different levels, increasing dimension of each set of swings, from A to E.

Group I. Standing

Starting position: standing with feet in stride position, body erect, arms at sides.

A. *Sway* body from L to R, flexing knees as weight is transferred from side to side. Body is relaxed, not stiff, so that there is slight drop as knees flex in front and slight lift as weight is held over either R or L foot.

| | 1 ct | |

7 more *swings* (making a total of 8), alternately L and R.

| | 7 cts | 8 cts |

B. *Swing* body to R, R arm stretching sideward to R side, knees flexing and then extending. Body remains facing forward, weight held on R foot at end of swing.

| | 1 ct | |

Swing body back to L, R arm swinging back to R side, knees flexing and then extending. 2nd half of swing receives less emphasis than 1st half, body swinging only slightly L of center.

| | 1 ct | |

6 more *swings* (making a total of 8), alternating 1st and 2nd half.

| | 6 cts | 8 cts |

C. *Repeat swings* to R and back to center, increasing dimension by stretching both arms to R side at about shoulder height on 1st half of swing.

| | 1 ct | |

Swing both arms down in front of body on 2nd half of swing.

| | 1 ct | |

6 more *swings* (making a total of 8), alternating 1st and 2nd half.

| | 6 cts | 8 cts |

D. *Swing* body and arms downward and then up to R side, both arms stretched overhead beside ears, knees flexing and then extending. Body remains facing forward, weight held over R foot at end of swing.

| | 1 ct | |

Swing body and arms downward and then up to L side, both arms stretching overhead beside ears, knees flexing and then extending. Body remains facing forward, weight held over L foot at end of swing.

| | 1 ct | |

6 more *swings* (making a total of 8), alternately R and L.

| | 6 cts | 8 cts |

E. *Swing* body and arms downward and then up to R side, both arms stretching overhead beside ears, knees flexing and then extending. Body remains facing forward, weight held over R foot at end of swing, L leg lifted sideward to L in extended position.

| | 1 ct | |

Swing body and arms downward and slightly to L of center, weight transferring to L foot.

| | 1 ct | |

6 more *swings* (making a total of 8), alternating 1st and 2nd half.

| | 6 cts | 8 cts |

Group II. Kneeling

Starting position: kneel stand, body erect over knees, arms at sides.
Increase dimension of each set of swings, from A to E.

Movements A, B, C, D are performed in exactly the manner described for Group I, with range of movement limited by kneeling base.		32 cts
E. *Swing* body and arms downward and then up to R side, placing R hand on floor at R side, L arm swinging overhead, knees flexing and then extending. Body remains facing forward; weight is held over R knee and R hand, L leg lifted sideward to L in extended position.	1 ct	
Swing body and arms back to center, arms returning to sides, weight transferred to both knees.	1 ct	
6 more *swings* (making a total of 8), alternating 1st and 2nd half of swing.	6 cts	8 cts

13. SWINGS

Meter varies for each group.

4 groups: 2 kneeling, 2 standing. Each group does 1 swing alone.
Then all 4 groups move together for 30 cts or 15 meas. of $\frac{6}{8}$ meter.

Group I 15 2-beat swings	30 cts
Group II 10 3-beat swings	30 cts
Group III 7½ 4-beat swings	30 cts
Group IV 6 5-beat swings	30 cts

Group I. Kneeling

Starting position: kneel stand, body erect over knees, arms overhead.

A. *Swing* body and arms downward, flexing at hips and rounding back.	1 ct	
B. *Swing* body and arms upward to starting position.	1 ct	2 cts

Group II. Kneeling

Starting position: same as for Group I.

A. *Swing* body and arms downward, flexing at hips and rounding back.	1 ct	
B. *Swing* body and arms upward to starting position.	1 ct	
C. *Swing* arms downward and backward, circling to overhead position, chest lifting as arms move back, head dropping slightly back.	1 ct	3 cts

Group III. Standing

Starting position: standing with feet together, body erect, arms overhead.

A. *Swing* body and arms downward, knees flexing and then extending, back rounding.	1 ct

B. *Swing* body and arms upward to starting position, knees flexing and then extending, back extending. — 1 ct

C. *Swing* body and arms diagonally downward to R, stepping R foot to side into stride position. Swing continues out to R and overhead. — 1 ct

D. *Repeat* swing to L, omitting step. (These last 2 swings form a figure 8.) — 1 ct   4 cts

Group IV. Standing

Starting position: standing with feet in stride position, body erect, R arm extended sideward at shoulder height, L arm at side.

A. *Swing* body and R arm to L, knees flexing and then extending, R arm stretching overhead. — 1 ct

B. *Swing* body and R arm downward and then up to R, knees flexing and then extending, R arm returning to starting position. — 1 ct

C. *Swing* body and R arm downward to center and then push up with R arm and body toward ceiling, knees flexing and then extending. — 1 ct

D. *Swing* body and R arm downward, knees flexing and then extending, back rounding. — 1 ct

E. *Swing* body and both arms upward, knees flexing and then extending, back extending, both arms stretching overhead. — 1 ct   5 cts

14. SWING, FALL, AND RECOVERY

10 meas. of $\frac{4}{4}$ meter.

3 groups: in canon form, each group starting 4 cts after previous group, and each group doing whole pattern through twice.

Starting position: standing with feet together, body erect, arms overhead.

A. *Swing* body and arms down, knees flexing and then extending, back rounding. — 1 ct

B. *Swing* body and arms up, knees flexing and then extending, back extending. — 1 ct

C. *Repeat* swing downward. — 1 ct

D. *Repeat* swing upward, lifting from floor with hop on R foot, L leg flexed at knee, lifted behind body. — 1 ct

E. *Fall* onto back by flexing at hips and knees, keeping weight forward over R foot. As L foot and lower leg touch floor, hands slide diagonally backward and body unrolls backward on floor. (Knees do not touch floor in falling.) Position at end of fall is extended back-lying position on floor, with R leg extended and L leg flexed at knee with outside of lower leg on floor, L foot crossed under R knee. — 2 cts   6 cts

A. *Recover:* roll to L into prone-lying position, R hip initiating movement, L leg remaining flexed at knee. — 1 ct

B. *Continue* roll to L, L leg lifted from hip with flexed knee, to lead roll. — 1 ct

C. *Continue* to hurdle sit with L leg flexed in front of body.	1 ct	
D. *Kneel* on L knee, back to audience.	1 ct	
E. *Stand* on R foot, pivoting in place slowly and bringing feet together, facing audience.	2 cts	6 cts

Note: Recovery should be executed as a single sustained movement, not as 5 separate movements.

LOCOMOTOR MOVEMENT

Locomotor movements are performed in 4 groups, each performing in turn. The groups remain constant; that is, the dancers in Group I always remain in Group I. Group I starts in downstage L corner, Group II in downstage R corner. These groups move back and forth across the downstage space (1st diagram). They alternate from R to L stage on each pattern performed. Group III starts in upstage L corner and moves diagonally downstage toward R side of stage. Group IV starts in upstage R corner and moves diagonally downstage toward L side of stage. These 2 groups move alternately from R or L corner (2nd diagram). In this way, the activity of each group is made clearly visible and the stage space is used to best advantage.

Whenever the above directional pattern is varied, it will be so indicated in the directions given on the following pages. Unless otherwise indicated, the starting position is always standing with feet together, body erect, arms at sides.

I. JUMPS

8 meas. of $\frac{4}{4}$ meter.

Group I

4 *foot bounces* in place. Toes do not leave floor; body erect.	4 cts	
4 small *jumps.* Feet leave floor, extended in the air; body erect.	4 cts	8 cts

Group II

4 *jumps* in place (as described above).	4 cts	
4 *jumps,* turning ¼ turn on each jump, making 1 full turn.	4 cts	8 cts

Group III

4 *jumps* in place.	4 cts	
4 *jumps,* turning ½ turn on each jump, making 2 full turns.	4 cts	8 cts

Group IV

4 *jump-leaps,* turning ¼ turn on each leap, making 1 full turn. Jump-leap consists of taking off from both feet (jump) and landing on R foot (leap) with L leg lifted in back in extended position.		8 cts

2. SLIDES AND JUMPS

24 meas. of ⅜ meter. (See comment on ⅜ meter, p. 151.)

Group I

3 *slides* and 1 *jump* with feet together, moving diagonally upstage to R, with R leg leading.	4 cts	
3 *slides* and 1 *jump* with feet together, moving diagonally downstage to L, with L leg leading, ending in starting position.	4 cts	8 cts

Group II

3 *slides* and 1 *jump* with feet together, making ½ turn on jump, moving diagonally upstage to L, with L leg leading.	4 cts	
3 *slides* and 1 *jump* with feet together, making ½ turn on jump, moving diagonally downstage to R, with L leg leading.	4 cts	8 cts

Group III

3 *slides* and 1 *jump* with feet together, making ¼ turn on jump, moving toward R stage, R leg leading.	4 cts	
Repeat pattern 3 more times, turning continually to R on ¼ turns, making a hollow square on the floor. Turns should be made sharply for clear change of direction.	12 cts	16 cts

Group IV

Repeat pattern of Group III, making a full turn in the air on each of the 4 jumps before starting slides in new direction. Turns should be made sharply for clear change of direction.		16 cts

3. WALKS AND WALK COMBINATIONS

74 meas. of ¼ meter.

Group I

16 *walks* forward, arms extended sideward at shoulder height.	16 cts

Group II

16 *walks* backward, arms extended sideward at shoulder height.	16 cts

Group III

4 *walks* forward, body in complete extension.	4 cts	
Pivot (½ turn) sharply on *and* ct after ct 4.		
4 *walks* backward, body flexed forward over knees, back rounded. The backward walks continue in the same line of direction as the forward walks, that is, downstage toward R side of stage.	4 cts	8 cts
Repeat walks forward and backward.		8 cts

Group IV

4 *walks* forward, body in extension, flexing forward after 4th step.   4 cts

4 *walks* turning, continuing same line of direction. Body extends gradually from flexed and rounded position; full extension is reached at end of 4th turning step. This is a spiral turn, body moving from low to high on the turn.   4 cts   8 cts

Repeat 4 walks forward and 4 walks turning.   8 cts

Group I

4 *walks* forward, stepping on whole foot, with knees flexed.   4 cts

4 *walks* forward, stepping on toes, with knees extended.   4 cts   8 cts

Repeat.   8 cts

Group II

4 *walks* forward, stepping on toes, with knees extended.   4 cts

4 *walks* turning in place, stepping on whole foot, with knees flexed.   4 cts   8 cts

Body is completely extended on toe-steps.

Repeat.   8 cts

Group III

4 *walks* forward, stepping on toes, with knees extended, bouncing through the arch of the foot on each step.   4 cts

4 *walks* turning, continuing same line of direction, stepping on toes, with knees extended, omitting bounce.   4 cts   8 cts

Repeat.   8 cts

Group IV

4 *walks* forward, stepping on toe of R foot, whole L foot.   4 cts

4 *walks* turning, continuing same line of direction, stepping on toe of R foot, whole L foot.   4 cts   8 cts

Body is completely extended on toe-steps.

Repeat.   8 cts

Group I

16 *walks* forward, preceding each step after the 1st by a tap with ball of foot: step R, tap L, step L, tap R, etc.   32 cts

Group II

16 *walks* forward, preceding each step after the 1st by a tap with ball of foot (as described for Group I). Step with R foot is taken diagonally forward and sideward to R; step with L foot is taken diagonally forward and sideward to L; so that pattern moves from side to side as well as forward.   32 cts

Group III

3 *steps* and 1 *tap,* moving diagonally forward to R: step sideward
   to R with R foot, step with L foot across in front of R, step sideward to R with R foot, tap with L beside R.   4 cts
Repeat, starting with L, moving on L diagonal.   4 cts   8 cts
Repeat, starting first with R foot and then with L foot.   8 cts

Group IV

3 *steps* and 1 *tap,* moving diagonally forward to R (as described for
   Group III).   4 cts
Repeat to L, making 1 full turn on 3 steps.   4 cts   8 cts
Repeat to R and repeat turn to L.   8 cts

Group III

Repeat pattern described above to R. Rhythmic pattern:

                    step   cross   step   tap

                     ♩.   ♪   ♩   ♩   4 cts

4 *"cat-steps"* to L. ("Cat-step" consists of sideward leap to L with
   L foot, step R across L). Rhythmic pattern:

                     leap   cross

                      ♪   ♪.   4 cts   8 cts

Pattern for 2 meas.:

step cross step tap leap   cross leap cross leap cross leap cross

 ♩.   ♪   ♩   ♩.♫ | ♩.♫   ♩.♫   ♩.♫   ♩

Repeat pattern 2 more times to center of stage, while Group IV
   walks to center of stage to meet Group III.   16 cts

Groups III and IV

Both groups move together in center of stage.

A. 3 *steps* and *hold* sideward to R, making 1 full turn to R on 3 steps.   4 cts
   Repeat to L.   4 cts   8 cts
   Note: Movement is very small and light; steps should be small
   and restrained.
B. 3 *steps* and *hold* sideward to R, making 1 full turn to R on 3 steps.   4 cts
   Repeat to L.   4 cts   8 cts
   Note: Movement is very large and heavy; steps should be large
   and knees well flexed, movement reaching out.
Repeat movements A and B.   16 cts
Groups III and IV then move back to starting places in their respec-
   tive corners.

4. PRANCES*

20 meas. of $\frac{4}{4}$ meter.

Group I

16 *prances* in place, knees flexed and legs lifted high in front.   16 cts

Group II

16 *prances* in place, knees extended and legs lifted high in front.   16 cts

Group III

16 *prances* moving forward, alternating 4 prances with knees flexed
(as for Group I), 4 prances with knees extended (as for Group II).   16 cts

Group IV

3 *prances* sideward to R, knees flexed, legs lifted high in front.	3 cts	
3 *prances* sideward to L, knees flexed, legs lifted high in front.	3 cts	
4 *prances* forward, knees extended, legs lifted high in front, hands clapping overhead on cts 1 and 3.	4 cts	10 cts
Repeat all 3 more times.		30 cts

5. SKIPS AND SKIP COMBINATIONS

58 meas. of $\frac{6}{8}$ meter.

Groups I and II

Both groups move simultaneously, each in its own corner of the
stage.

8 *skips* forward.		8 cts
8 *skips* backward to place.		8 cts
4 *skips* sideward, toward center of stage.	4 cts	
4 *skips* sideward, toward respective corners.	4 cts	8 cts
4 *skips* sideward, toward center of stage.	4 cts	
4 *skips* backward, to respective corners.	4 cts	8 cts

Group III

4 *skips* forward.	4 cts	
4 *skips* turning in place.	4 cts	8 cts
Repeat.		8 cts

Group IV

4 *skips* forward.	4 cts	
4 *skips* turning, continuing same line of direction; body alternately in extension and flexion on these 4 turning skips.	4 cts	8 cts
Repeat.		8 cts

---

*See description in Glossary.

Group III

4 *skips* forward.	4 cts	
4 *skips* turning backward to place.	4 cts	8 cts

2 slow *"cat-steps"* (see Group III under Walks) to L. Rhythmic pattern:

leap	cross	leap	cross		
♪	♩.	♪	♩.	4 cts	

4 fast *"cat-steps"* to L. Rhythmic pattern:

leap	cross	leap	cross	leap	cross	leap	cross		
♪	♪.	♪	♪.	♪	♪.	♪	♪.	4 cts	8 cts

4 *skips* backward to place.		4 cts

Group IV

2 1-legged *skips forward.* (One-legged skip is a step-hop-step with repetition always on the same foot. The rhythm is	4 cts	
3 *jumps* in place, and 1 *leap* diagonally forward to R, onto R foot, body leaning over R leg.	4 cts	8 cts
1 *leap* forward onto L foot; *hold* position.	2 cts	
1 *leap* backward onto R foot; *hold* position.	2 cts	4 cts
1 *hop* on R foot and 3 *slides* to L.	3 cts	
1 *jump* with feet together, making ½ turn.	1 ct	4 cts
Repeat all back to place.		16 cts

6. COMBINATION AXIAL AND LOCOMOTOR MOVEMENTS

6 meas. of $\frac{4}{4}$ meter.

All 4 groups move together, remaining in their own starting places.

Groups I and II

4 *jump-leaps* (small) in place. (See Group IV under Jumps.) 1st jump-leap is toward center of stage; succeeding jump-leaps alternate toward outside and center.	8 cts	
Hold starting position	8 cts	16 cts
2 *jump-leaps* (small) in place, facing alternately toward center and outside of stage.	4 cts	
Hold starting position.	4 cts	8 cts

Groups III and IV

4 *jump-leaps* (large) in place, facing alternately toward center and outside of stage.	8 cts	
2 circular *body swings* (large), starting alternately toward center and outside of stage. (See Group I under Sustained and Percussive Movement.)	8 cts	16 cts

2 *jump-leaps* (large) facing alternately toward center and outside
    of stage.   4 cts

2 down and up 2-beat *swings* (small and fast). (See Swing, Fall, and
    Recovery.)   4 cts   8 cts

7. RUNS AND LEAPS

16 meas. of $\frac{4}{4}$ meter; then 32 meas. of $\frac{3}{4}$ meter.

Group I

16 *"rocking" steps* (small) forward, R foot leading. "Rocking" step
consists of a very small leap onto leading foot (R), with body
rocking slightly forward, and a small run on back foot (L), which
is brought up to leading foot but not beyond it, while body rocks
slightly backward. Movement should be light and bouncing.   16 cts

Group II

16 *"rocking"* steps (larger) forward, R foot leading.   16 cts

Group III

8 *leap-runs* forward, R foot leading. Leap-run is greatly extended
"rocking" step; leap is always onto R foot; run is always with L
foot, which passes leaping foot rather than remaining in back as
it does in "rocking" step.   16 cts

Group IV

Repeat pattern of Group III.   16 cts

Group III

8 *leap-run-runs* forward, alternating feet on leaps.   24 cts

Group IV

8 *leap-run-runs* forward, alternating feet on leaps.   24 cts

Group III

8 *leap-run-runs* forward, alternating feet on leaps.   24 cts

Group IV

8 *leap-run-runs* forward, alternating feet on leaps.   24 cts

Bibliography

DANCE CHOREOGRAPHY

Ellfeldt, Lois, *A Primer for Choreographers.* Palo Alto, Calif.: National Press Books, 1967.

Hawkins, Alma, *Creating Through Modern Dance.* Englewood Cliffs, N.J.: Prentice-Hall, 1964.

Horst, Louis, *Pre-Classic Dance Forms.* New York: Kamin Dance Publishers, 1953.

Horst, Louis and Carroll Russell, *Modern Dance Forms.* San Francisco: Impulse Publications, 1961.

Humphrey, Doris, *The Art of Making Dances.* New York: Holt, Rinehart and Winston, 1959.

Joyce, M., *First Steps in Teaching Creative Dance.* Palo Alto, California, National Press Books, 1973.

DANCE HISTORY

DeMille, Agnes, *The Book of the Dance.* New York: Golden Press, 1963.

Kirsten, Lincoln, *Dance* (a short history of classical theatrical dancing). Brooklyn, N.Y.: Dance Horizons, Inc., 1969.

————, *Movement and Metaphor.* New York: Praeger Publishers, 1970.

Krause, Richard, *History of the Dance.* Englewood Cliffs, N.J.: Prentice-Hall, 1969.

Martin, John, *Introduction to the Dance.* Brooklyn, N.Y.: Dance Horizons, 1965.

Percival, John, *Modern Ballet.* New York: E. P. Dutton & Co., 1970.

Sachs, Curt, *World History of the Dance.* New York: W. W. Norton Co., Inc., 1937.

Sorrell, Walter, *The Dance Through the Ages.* New York: Grosset & Dunlap, 1967.

DANCE TEACHING

Cheyney, Gay and Janet Strader, *Modern Dance.* Boston: Allyn & Bacon, 1969.

Jones, Ruth and Margaret DeHaan, *Modern Dance in Education.* New York: Teachers College, Columbia University, 1948.

Lockhart, Aileene and Esther Pease, *Modern Dance* (Building and Teaching Lessons). Dubuque, Iowa: Wm. C. Brown Co., 1966.

Norris, Dorothy and Reva Shiner, *Keynotes to Modern Dance.* Minneapolis: Burgess Publishing Co., 1969.

Radir, Ruth, *Modern Dance for the Youth of America.* New York: A. G. Barnes & Co., 1944.

Shurr, Gertrude and Rachel D. Yocum, *Modern Dance—Technique and Teaching.* New York: A.G. Barnes & Co., 1949.

MODERN DANCE
(BACKGROUND AND HISTORY)

Cohen, Selma Jean, *Dance as a Theatre Art.* New York: Dodd-Mead, 1974.

Cohen, Selma Jean (ed.), *The Modern Dance (Seven Statements of Belief).* Middleton, Conn.: Wesleyan University Press, 1965.

Maynard, Olga, *American Modern Dancers.* Boston: Little, Brown & Co., 1965.

McDonagh, Don, *Martha Graham.* New York: Praeger Publishers, 1973.

Walker, Katherine Sorley, *Dance and Its Creators.* New York: John Day Co., 1972.

RELATED FIELDS

The Four Seasons, Haiku Harvest, Japanese Haiku. Mount Vernon, N.Y.: Peter Pauper Press, 1958, 1962.

Brook, Peter, *The Empty Space*. New York: Atheneum, 1968.

Hall, James B. and Barry Ulanov, *Modern Culture and the Arts*. New York: McGraw-Hill, 1972.

Hunt, Douglas and Kari, *Pantomime*. New York: Atheneum, 1968.

King, Nancy, *Theatre Movement: The Actor and His Space*. New York: Drama Book Specialists/Publishers, 1971.

Read, Herbert, *The Origins of Form in Art*. New York: Horizon Press, 1965.

Reische, Diana (ed.), *The Performing Arts in America*. New York: H.W. Wilson Co., 1973.

Rockefeller Bros. Fund, *The Performing Arts—Problems and Prospects*. New York: McGraw-Hill, 1965.

Selden, Samuel, *The Stage in Action*. New York: Appleton-Century, 1941.

White, Charles L., *Drums Through the Ages*. Los Angeles: The Sterling Press, 1960.

ACCOMPANIMENT

Throughout the text, specific records have been suggested for specific creative studies. Local music and record shops can usually order records and will also have current albums appropriate to dance composition. Students will often wish to bring in their own records or tapes to use in class.

The following sources will mail catalogs upon request:

Educational Records Sales
200 W. Wrightwood
Elmhurst, Ill. 60126

500 South Douglas St.
El Segundo, Ca. 90245

157 Chambers St.
New York, New York 10007

Kimbo Records
Box 55
Deal, N. J. 07723

The Record Center
2581 Piedmont Rd., N.E.
Atlanta, Ga. 30224
(Phys. Ed. Catalog)

Russell Records, Inc.
P.O. Box 3318
Ventura, Ca.

W. Schwann Inc.
137 Newbury St.
Boston, Mass. 02116

RECORDS

These are a few suggestions for background accompaniment or composition.

"Beat That Drum"
Sandy Nelson
Imperial 12231

"Electronic Music"
Turnabout 34046S

"Environments"
Synonics Research, Inc.
Atlantic Recording Corp.
1841 Broadway
N.Y., N.Y. 10023
        Disc 1—The Psychologically Ultimate Seashore
                Optimum Aviary
        Disc 2—Tintinnabulation
                Dawn at New Hope, Pa.
        Disc 3—Be-In
                Dusk at New Hope, Pa.

"In Sound From Way Out"
Vanguard VSD 79222

"Jazz Raga"
Gabor Szabo
Impulse A 9128

"Let There Be Drums"
Sandy Nelson
Imperial 9159

"Modern Jazz Movement"
Kimbo Records 4080

"N.Y. Export—Jazz"
Warner Bros. 1240

"The Passions"
Les Baxter
Capitol LAL 486

"The Percussions of Strausbourg"
Limelight 586051

"Tone Poems in Color"
Capitol Records W735

INDEX

Other fine books available from Jalmar Press